Contents

Revolt in the West

The Western Rebellion of 1549

John Sturt

DEVON BOOKS

First published in Great Britain in 1987 by Devon Books
Copyright © John Sturt
ISBN 0 86114-776-6

ACKNOWLEDGEMENTS
Illustrations are reproduced by kind permission of the following:

Miss Emily Clay (pp. 23, 27)
Exeter City Council/Devon Record Office (p. 60–61)
The Mansell Collection (p.41)
Westcountry Studies Library (p. 6, 16, 46, 53, 87)

Cover picture by courtesy of the Westcountry Studies Library.

Line drawings on pp. 77, 91, and 97 by the author.

British Library Cataloguing-in-Publication Data

Sturt, John
    Revolt in the west: the Western Rebellion of 1549.
    1. Revolutions——England——Exeter (Devon)——History——16th century
    2. Exeter (Devon)——History
    I. Title
    942.3′5605′3   DA690.E9

Printed and bound in Great Britain by A. Wheaton & Co. Ltd.

DEVON BOOKS

Official Publisher to Devon County Council
Devon Books is a division of A. Wheaton & Co. Ltd, which represents:

Editorial, Design, Publicity, Production and Manufacturing
A. Wheaton & Co. Ltd
Hennock Road, Marsh Barton, Exeter, Devon EX2 8RP
Tel: 0392 74121; Telex 42749 (WHEATN G)
(A. Wheaton & Co. Ltd is a member of the Pergamon/B.P.C.C. Group of
Companies)

Sales and Distribution
Town & Country Books, P.O. Box 31, Newton Abbot, Devon TQ12 5AQ
Tel: 080 47 2690

Introduction

In June 1549 Henry VIII had been dead for two years. His eleven-year-old son Edward VI was an invalid, and the nation's affairs were in the control of Edward Seymour, the Duke of Somerset, who was the uncle of the young king and held the title of Lord Protector. There was widespread dissatisfaction throughout the country, because unpopular land reforms had been introduced, the dissolution of the monasteries had not worked out as the people had hoped, and the religious reforms decreed by King Henry years earlier were about to be enforced.

There were risings or serious disturbances in fourteen other counties in 1549, but it was left to the people of Devon and Cornwall to march in full-scale revolt for the sake of the old religion and the old ways. The tin miners of Cornwall and the farm labourers of Devon armed themselves as best they could and found the leadership they needed. The drama was played out in the fields and villages of Devon. Within a few weeks the West Country was in flames and the city of Exeter under heavy siege. The conflict was sustained against the king's professional army and regiments of foreign mercenaries through the unbelievable bravery and determination of simple country folk who were not prepared to be dictated to from London.

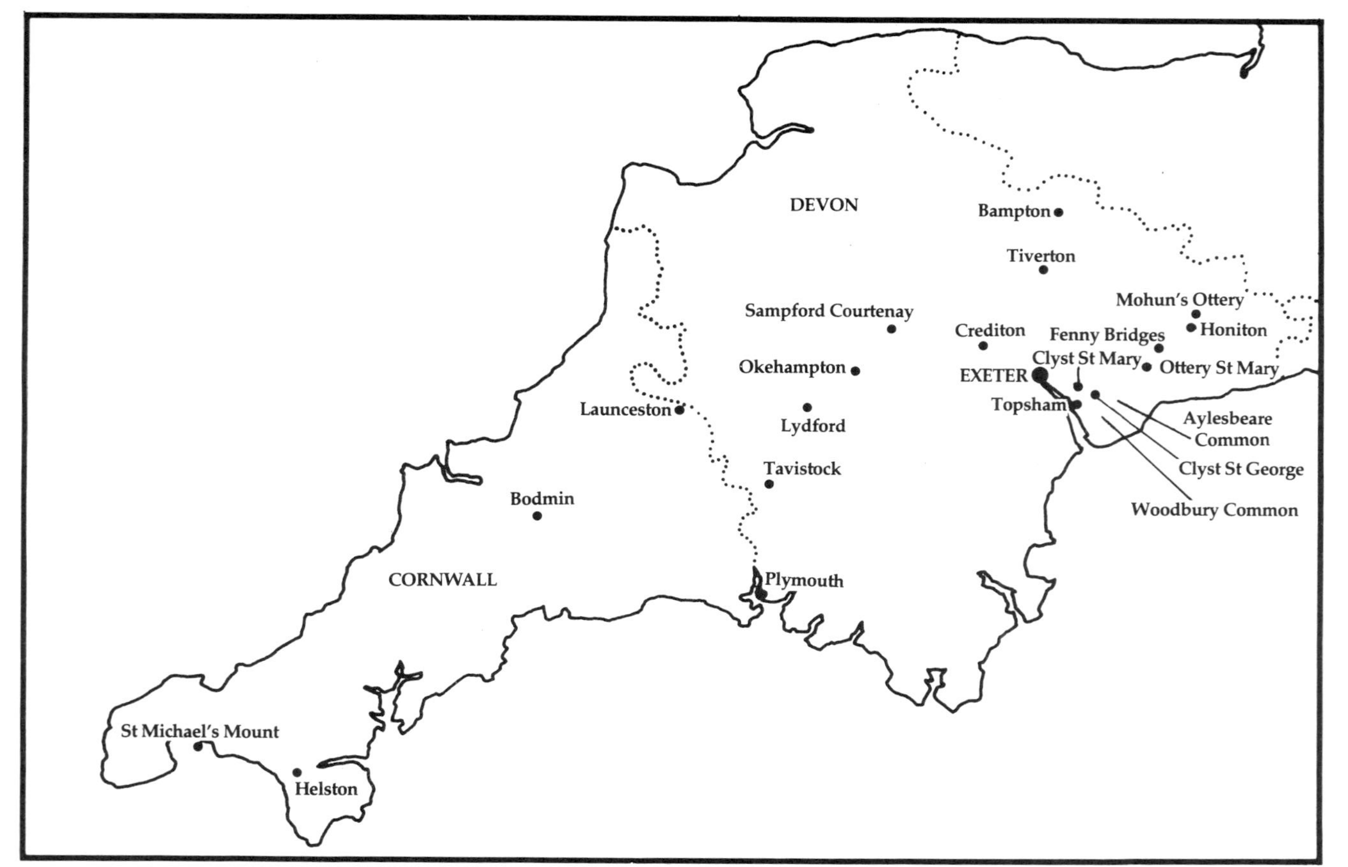
DEVON
Bampton
Tiverton
Mohun's Ottery
Sampford Courtenay
Crediton
Fenny Bridges
Honiton
Clyst St Mary
Okehampton
EXETER
Ottery St Mary
Topsham
Aylesbeare
Common
Clyst St George
Launceston
Lydford
Woodbury Common
Tavistock
Bodmin
Plymouth
CORNWALL
St Michael's Mount
Helston

—1—
The Seeds of Discontent

The Western Rebellion of 1549 has been described as the most formidable opposition to the Reformation that England saw. It was almost entirely a rural movement and its three causes deserve examination.

To understand the dramatic reactions to the hated land reforms it is necessary to be aware of the economic plight of the country and the desperate position the poor people found themselves in. In his vigorous youth Henry VIII had governed strongly and wisely; he laid the foundations of a modern England, created the Royal Navy and a system of dockyards, and gave the country a chance of international prosperity. In his gloomy and bloody old age things had not gone well for England. At his death the country was in the grip of inflation, with a debased currency, and landlords able to dictate the level of wages. The nation would have to wait for the shrewdness, scepticism and courage of Elizabeth I before the lot of the common man would improve. Meanwhile, the glaring examples of extravagance at court only underlined to the poor people that, for them at least, times were hard.

The trouble with the land reforms was that they tended to dispossess only small farmers. They pleased, and were designed to please, those who owned land on a large scale, but did nothing for those who worked on it. The Inclosure Acts benefited sheep farmers in particular but oppressed the peasants. Many of the latter were still villeins, tied workers, and they too would have to wait for Elizabeth for their emancipation (she, characteristically, forced many of them to buy their freedom, at her price).

The second cause of popular unrest centred on the dissolution of the monasteries, and more recently of the chantries and guilds. At the chantries one was able to pay for prayers in perpetuity for the souls of the dead and Henry had let it be known that he was 'suppressing superstition' when he disbanded them. The guilds, also, had become very wealthy and were initially a popular target, but the destruction of these institutions, as with the monasteries, tended to enrich the court and courtiers and not the common man.

The dissolution of the monasteries had gone the same way. Originally Henry had three objectives in mind when he ordained the 'secularization' of monastic lands and properties. The first was the manifestation and evident acknowledgement of the new religion and his control over it; the second was the tapping of vast sources of wealth for the Crown and for the Crown's use, and the third was the enhancement of his popularity with ordinary citizens.

The first two of these went very much according to plan, though after Henry's death powerful men, like Somerset himself, siphoned off huge sums which would not have been within the royal calculations. Somerset House (and the original was much more of a palace than a house) was built entirely with the profits that accrued to the Duke from the dissolution. In fact the method of disposal of monastic lands did more for the royal plan than was perhaps realized, for it created a squirearchy owning, by purchase, land that had belonged to the religious houses, and thus had a built-in safeguard against re-establishment, based on the self-interest of the holders of the new manors.

Henry's third intention also looked, at the start, as if it was going to work. The people were told that the dissolution of the great monastic houses would benefit them financially: lands taken from greedy abbots would become common land, rents would either be reduced or held down, and life would blossom with the sacking of the wealthy and corrupt institutions that had been a burden on the poor for centuries.

In fact almost precisely the opposite happened. The estates of the monasteries were certainly re-allocated, but not in the way suggested. In the main they went to the Crown and were sold and resold down the line. Some went to buy loyalty to the Crown, or to pay debts owed by the Crown. Few ended up in any sort of common use or ownership.

But worse still, the land found its way into the hands of those who were determined to make the maximum profit out of it, and who proceeded to manage it with increased efficiency. Much of it went to people who did not live near their property and took on agents to make it pay. Many tenants found themselves paying higher rents than they had paid to the monks, and receiving a good deal less consideration and understanding of their problems. Some of this took time to happen. Many old monastic leases were allowed to run their course, but as time went by they were replaced by new leases at increased rents linked to oppressive fines for any late payment.

Of course it was not only the thought of financial advantage that made the dissolution popular with the poorer people at the outset. It had been widely advertised as a key part of the king's new war on superstition and corruption. What G. M. Trevelyan in his *History of England* calls 'the grosser forms of superstition and pious fraud' were to be put down. The worship of images, reverence for relics of the saints, the sale of pardons, miracle-working statues, and any other evidence of the power of Rome were to be abolished in the king's name, and society was to be the better for it.

And no doubt it was, but as well as corrupt monks there were those who distributed charity to the very poor and distressed; and if in general the monks were inefficient landlords, they were also less severe and exacting in that capacity than those who now held the land. The poor were poorer for the dissolution, and the very poor were starving.

What seemed doubly unfair was that the people's only real consolation in their misery – the old, familiar form of religious services – was now also to be taken from them, apparently. The obligatory changes in church ritual and the enforced use of English in place of Latin, as laid out in the new service-book (known as the *First Prayer Book of Edward VI*) were to be the third and most immediate cause of the 1549 rebellion.

When Henry VIII and Cranmer, the first Protestant Archbishop of Canterbury, had worked out the reforms in religious observance that were considered necessary, they genuinely felt that they were acting with moderation. Not only were the reforms far from sweeping, but they were to be phased in gradually and not fully insisted upon for nearly twenty years. In his will Henry had laid down that the new measures should be enforced only in 1561, when Edward reached the age of royal competence, which was reckoned to be twenty-four.

In his attempts at moderation, however, Henry had left a time bomb ticking away into his son's short reign. In many parts of England Whit Sunday 1549 was of limited importance, for most or all of the reforms had already been introduced in the time allowed, and the government's new deadline of 9 June was of interest, but little more. But two factors made the situation in the south-western counties very different.

The first was the particular devoutness and conservatism of the people of this region, whose lives centred very much on their churches and their priests. Their religion seemed particularly important to them now that their other rights and their relative prosperity had been swept away. The drab daily routine and the dullness and hardship of home life had up to now been alleviated by the warmth and beauty of the old-style ritual at church. To lose that also seemed to many of them too much to bear.

The second point was that, in the West Country, all the changes would

Edward VI

have to happen at once. In such remote parts of the kingdom very few alterations had been made in church routine, because neither the priests nor the people wanted them and because orders from London were neither immediately nor instinctively obeyed. The clergy had been able to look with relative equanimity on the attacks on the abbeys, for there was always rivalry between those in holy orders who ministered to and lived among the people and those who prayed for them in protected and secluded orders. At the suggestion that the litany should be reformed, however, they were filled with a sense of outrage and quite ready to encourage their congregations to react likewise.

In the churches of the West, little or nothing had yet happened to alter the age-old proceedings. Henry had not insisted on the changes being made, and no one of any importance had visited the churches to press the clergy to do so. They suddenly found themselves backed up against the deadline of 9 June with everything due to change overnight.

To the Cornishmen there seemed a special injustice in laws that stipulated English as the language of the mass and the prayer-book from Whit Sunday onwards. At that time a great majority of them spoke only their own Celtic tongue and did not even understand English.

Cornwall was still simmering over events of the year before, when a wildly unpopular and thoroughly nasty Royal Commissioner (also ensconced as an entirely bogus archdeacon) was killed as he was engaged in ripping the villagers' beloved statues out of the parish church at Helston as part of the new policies of reformation. The brutality with which that affray had been punished was a prime cause of the next and much more serious one.

From the government's point of view the build-up of discord and dissent was an acute embarrassment. When it eventually flared into armed rebellion they were desperate to attribute the trouble to discontent over land reforms and not to religious disquiet. If the trouble could be attributed to a political cause, there was a possibility of defusing it by a change in political strategy – or, more likely, by the promise of such a change. It would also distract the rest of the country from the religious issue.

Above all, the government had to limit the discontent to the South West. Their forces were fully stretched by wars in France, and against the Scots, and they had little in reserve to deal with what they feared most, a resurgence of the Pilgrimage of Grace, now twelve years past but frighteningly fresh in everyone's memory. If that were to happen the North and East of the kingdom would be likely to rise with the men of the western counties and it was more than doubtful that the government could have retained control.

From its title it is clear that the Pilgrimage of Grace was fundamentally a religious protest, though social injustice and insensitive officialdom also contributed to the conflagration. It started in the far North. Royal Commissioners, busy implementing the king's policy in regard to the dissolution of the monasteries, had made a lordly and overweening progress through most of Northumberland. But they found that the monks of Hexham Abbey were of sterner stuff than most. They confronted the Commissioners with longbow and crossbow and sent them packing with the loss, if not actually of life, then certainly of dignity. At this, trouble broke out all over the North and East, culminating in a massive rising in Lincolnshire. Promises and assurances temporarily allayed this strong feeling, but when the promises were retracted there developed a great ground swell of rebellion, based in Yorkshire.

The Pilgrimage of Grace grew out of this first trouble in 1536. The northerners' plan was to march to London behind their crosses and religious banners and present their case to the king and court. It was to be a peaceful protest against the new interference in religion. This was an early example of civil disobedience and perhaps the first attempt in this country to put grievances before a government without threat of violence or display of disloyalty.

That the men who led the Pilgrimage were honourable and intent on reconciliation meant little to a king who was neither when it did not suit him. Promises were broken, safe conducts abrogated and a terrible vengeance taken in blood. Henry broke the northerners with the brutality of his revenge, but he never forgot that they raised forty thousand armed men at Doncaster in a few days. And, when they saw that the banner behind which the men of the Western Rebellion marched was the same as that used in the Pilgrimage of Grace, Henry's successors trembled for the safety of the realm.

—2—

The English Reformation

Early in 1549 the average countryman in the West of England would have known little of the English Reformation. He would have known that the late King Harry had become head of the Church in place of the pope in Rome, but little would have changed in his parish and he would have been quite likely to applaud the change in Church leadership. At that time the tide of anti-clericalism was directed against the monasteries and chantries and not against parish priests. He would have suffered hardship in the wake of the dissolution, but he was used to hardship.

Until quite recently the South West had been unusually prosperous, enjoying the full flowering of the wool trade. These were the days when so many West Country churches were enlarged and made more splendid. Most of the sheep may have belonged to rich men, but at certain times of the year the care of sheep is labour-intensive, and there were many jobs allied to the wool trade, such as tucking and fulling and weaving. Some contemporary accounts also suggest that there were more sheep in Devonshire than in any other county. Although the Reformation may scarcely have touched our countryman, we need to have a picture of it to put later events in perspective.

It was really in the reign of Henry VIII that the foundations of modern England were laid, and there were more complex reasons for the Reformation than just a king wanting a divorce which a pope declined to grant. The tide of change from the medieval into the modern age is shown by many things besides the religious break with Rome. This was the era in which the seeds of our sea power were sown, when heavy cannon were first mounted in the body of a ship (at Henry's own insistence) and the tactics of naval warfare finally ceased to be those of the ancient Greeks and Romans. It was also the era in which Parliament began to be a force to be reckoned with in the country, and the ancient universities of Oxford and Cambridge broke free of the clerical stranglehold and started preparing lay undergraduates, the sons of gentlemen, for public service or a career at court. It was a time when English independence was established, in the face of European opposition, and the previously volatile nobles were finally subjugated to royal rule by Privy Council and Parliament. Because Henry was, in spirit, a modern and forward-looking monarch (like his father and his daughter Elizabeth) he eventually had to break with and destroy Cardinal Wolsey, who had been so useful to him even though, as a churchman and as a civil servant, he was a medievalist. It is wrong to assume that Henry quarrelled with Wolsey over the divorce. He dismissed him because his usefulness was spent and because in future he needed to look forward rather than back.

Luther's Reformation in Germany and the sack of Rome by the armies of Charles V, who ruled both Germany and Spain, conveniently paved the way for Henry's break. G. M. Trevelyan puts it thus: 'If ever there was a moment when European opinion made it easy for England to break with the Papacy, it was the generation that followed the revolt of Luther and the sack of Rome.' It can be argued with some conviction that Henry would have needed to make the break anyway, irrespective of the divorce question, though that certainly produced a convenient reason. In fact it was not really a divorce at all; it was more like an annulment. What Henry needed was a statement that he had never been free to marry Catherine of Aragon, since she had previously been married to his own brother. He wanted a declaration that an unlawful union, such as his, could be set aside; this would leave him free to remarry.

Nor was Pope Clement VII unwilling to oblige. There were plenty of precedents: he himself had recently released Henry's sister, the Queen of Scotland, from an inconvenient marriage, and with less reason. Earlier popes had released kings of France with no excuse at all. Clement would probably have been happy to accommodate Henry if he had been able to. But since the sack of Rome he was, if not actually the prisoner of Charles V, at least living under his 'protection', and Charles was Catherine of Aragon's nephew. Clement regretted that on this occasion he was powerless.

When this situation came to a head, England was just beginning to feel secure in naval and political terms. The tide of anti-clericalism was now strong enough to be felt, and the unpopularity of the great monastic houses was becoming apparent, with widespread rumours of corruption and misconduct within some monasteries. None of these events caused the others, yet they were all interrelated and mutually supporting.

The new nationalism made Henry question the necessity for England to look abroad for its laws. The emergent English Parliament suggested itself as a better route for legal decisions. The sacking of the monasteries did not depend on the break with Rome, but it was a convenient follow-up and coincided nicely with their unpopularity, which no doubt Henry's civil servants inflamed for him. It also fitted in with the anti-clerical feeling in the air, and with the disgrace and fall from power of Cardinal Wolsey, who had failed to obtain the divorce. Wolsey would have raised objections to Henry's break with Rome; in any case, Henry had no further use for him.

When he needed to turn popular opinion against the monastic houses Henry had no difficulty in doing so. Actual corruption and gross misconduct were probably quite rare, but there were instances of both, which, in view of their setting, were highly sensational. Abbots were great men and many of them sat in the House of Lords alongside the bishops, giving the Lords Spiritual a majority over the Lords Temporal, a majority that lasted until the dissolution. Being enormously wealthy landlords, the abbots could be seen to stand between the peasantry and any degree of prosperity, and when nationalism was developed even further by the break with Rome, it was easy to accuse them of being the troops and secret supporters of a foreign pope.

Whether Henry VIII really appreciated the true reasons why it was time to sweep away the monasteries it is not certain. He certainly saw them as a source of great wealth, he realized that it was logical and probably necessary to dissolve them after his breach with the papacy, and he was well aware that the new spirit of nationalism made the move a popular one. He also recognized the cogency of a new doctrine being expounded in Heidelberg by the philosopher Erastus, who held that it was essential for ecclesiastical power to be subject to political power if a country is to move forward and develop. This theory was tailor-made for Henry's circumstances, and suited his wish for dissolution. But Henry may not have understood the real justification for his action against the religious houses. He was probably too close to the issue, too greedy, too much advised by time-servers and sycophants to be as clear on the matter as his own intellect should have made him.

The real crime of the religious houses was more serious than the occasional scandal, the exploitation of superstition, the selling of absolution, the idleness and luxurious living. Even though these did occur, they were the exception and not the rule. In the main the inmates of abbeys and nunneries lived relatively virtuous lives of considerable comfort and made little impact on the world outside their walls. The fundamental charge against the religious houses was that they had become irrelevant and had lost their way.

No longer were the monks and nuns and their pensioners drawn from a fairly wide band of society – a surprisingly large number of them were the dependants of noblemen – and now they neither worked with their hands nor suffered the hardships of asceticism. No longer did the religious houses act as centres of learning and of intellectual life, or give a great part of their endowments to feed the poor and help the needy. They had become merely self-perpetuating, self-supporting establishments and were of little further use to society.

Other countries in Europe, in the aftermaths of their 'reformations', were dragged through protracted and bloody religious wars. Two things had spared England from bloodshed on a similar scale: the rule of a strong king, and the grudging acceptance of the changes by the 'lay clergy' (those who served the people and the parishes) from the bishops downwards.

By the time of the Western Rebellion the strong king was in his grave and a rather liberal and vacillating regent was in charge. The envy and enmity between the lay clergy and the now defunct monks and friars had ensured the acceptance of the Protestant Church in many parts of the kingdom, but not in the West Country, where the Duke of Somerset's determination to centralize all power in London was also resented.

The ordinary West Countryman knew almost nothing of all this. He knew that old King Harry had thumbed his nose at the Pope of Rome, and good luck to him. The monasteries had gone, and while he had thought that a good idea at first, he now realized that his new master paid lower wages and was stricter with him. If he was sick there was no longer a chance of alms from the abbey, and the price of bread and ale had gone up again, too.

He felt sorry for the monks. They had tiny pensions, of course, just about the same as he earned, but they had no idea how to eke them out. They had been used to a soft life and couldn't begin to snare a rabbit or steal a turnip. There was no suitable work for ex-monks and they had to drift from place to place, hoping for a charitable reception. He was sorry for them, but they were not his affair. He did care about his family, about getting enough food, and about the village church. That was why he was particularly annoyed by a rumour that had been going round recently about a new prayer-book. From next month, from June, the whole of the prayer-book was to be in English, and a lot of the good old mass too. The priest was not to be allowed to wear the proper vestments or carry out the old rituals. What was the use of a mass if it wasn't said properly? He had heard that a lot of the men in the village were not prepared to accept this change. Could they be forced to, in their own church? What had it got to do with London? If there was going to be a row about it he was going to join in. He could tell his priest was against the change; he had more or less said so on several occasions. People said there was a lot of trouble about it in Cornwall as well. He did not normally think a lot of those 'foreigners' down there, but if they were against it he would be with them. Those Cornish had a bit of a reputation for fighting and wrestling and so on. They would find that the Devon lads could fight too, if they had to.

—3—

Fury in the Far West

For Cornishmen the grievances were much the same, but since the majority of them spoke little English the replacement of the Latin prayer-book to which they were accustomed was an even greater blow than to the men of Devon. There seems also to have been an extra insensitivity on the part of the authorities in their choice of Commissioners and other agents of enforcement in Cornwall. Perhaps they were looked on as being more turbulent than the apparently placid Devonian peasantry; perhaps they were treated with more contempt because of the widespread use of their own language. In any event, it was clear that many of those who attended to the king's business in that county were noted for their high-handedness, their arrogance and both personal and professional greed.

To no one could this description be more accurately applied than William Body. Years earlier Body had been in the service of Cromwell, Lord Privy Seal and general 'fixer' for Henry VIII, and a person who had made himself indispensable to that unscrupulous man obviously had few scruples himself. There are references to accusations of theft and embezzlement years before, but either the evidence was inadequate or Body was too valuable to Cromwell for any action to be taken. In the 1530s he was sent to Ireland as a spy. He went on an expedition against the Irish Leader O'Brian led by the Lord Deputy of Ireland, Lord Grey, who complained in a letter about Body's drunken behaviour, abominable language and lies. Body, for his part, was furious with Lord Grey because of personal discomforts in the campaign. Getting no sympathy, he left 'in a grete fume', ominously swearing vengeance.

Vengeance was a strong suit with Body. Within a few months Lord Grey was to lay his head on the axeman's block on Tower Green. Body may have been a base and dishonest braggart, but in those days, if you had a great man's ear and were useful to him you might exact vengeance, however unjustified your complaint.

Late in 1537 Body embarked on a financial deal which was to bring him into contact with Cornwall and thus make him of interest to us here. He persuaded an impoverished divine called Wynter, thought to be an illegitimate son of Cardinal Wolsey, to lease him the Archdeaconry of Cornwall for thirty-three years, at thirty pounds a year. Body would receive all the dues and rents the archdeaconry commanded. For Wynter, the most important part of the bargain was that he would be paid a large portion of the rent in advance.

This arrangement was clearly unlawful. Body was not even in holy orders, so he was quite unqualified to act as archdeacon, but he had some bogus legal document drawn up and Wynter's qualms were soothed by the sight of the ready cash. He seems to have got away with it for several years. Repeated enquiries from the Bishop of Exeter were blandly ignored or fended off with pseudo-legal retorts. Then Body began to spend time in Cornwall collecting his dues. His boasts about being known as the 'hammer of the monks' while he had been helping Cromwell with the dissolution of the monasteries would not have increased his popularity even if he had been a better man than he was.

One day he was embroiled in a brawl in St Stephen's Church in Launceston, where his bluff was called by an elderly cleric. Body was jostled and fell to the ground. Conscious of the hostile mood of the meeting he left hurriedly, swearing vengeance. There are no records to tell us whether he was successful, but on another occasion he managed to sue two members of the Bishop of Exeter's staff. One of them was sent to prison, while the other was sentenced to death.

It was almost unbelievably clumsy of the authorities to choose Body to oversee a number of highly unpopular church reforms in Cornwall in 1547, but they did and he carried out his duties with such unusual arrogance that a local magistrate had him clapped in gaol for it. It seems likely that he was locked up for only a few days.

In April 1548 Body was appointed Royal Commissioner and put in charge of a mission to remove all statues and 'popery' from Cornwall's churches. He was by that time so unpopular in the county that people would spit on the ground at the mere mention of his name, but he undertook the mission with enthusiasm. Indeed, he seemed to welcome the chance of enraging and humiliating the Cornish and he made little secret of the fact.

On 5 April he was to deal with the church in Helston, a town where he was particularly unpopular. The bells were rung in reverse order in the surrounding parishes (an alarm signal common in those days) and a large crowd had assembled even before he arrived. A thousand people collected in the main square of Helston while Body was still at his iconoclastic work inside the church. On hearing the uproar he ran into a nearby house but was dragged out by the mob. His bodyguard did not lift a finger to intervene, which indicates how he was thought of even amongst the king's men. Body was killed by the knife of William Kylter, a priest, and local clergymen lectured the people on the rightness of what had been done.

John Ressiegh, a yeoman of Helston, made an impassioned speech from the steps of the market cross, and a proclamation was published. I quote the last few lines in its original form. It makes it clear that no one in Helston was unduly worried about Body's demise: '... that thei wolde haue all suche lawes as was made by the late Kynge Henry theight and none other, untyll the Kings Maiestie that now is accomplish thage of xxiiij yeres, and that whoso defende Body or follow such new faschyons as he dyd thei wolde punyshe him lykewise'.

By the next day the crowd in Helston numbered nearly three thousand and the county was at flash-point. Just in time the king's messenger arrived with a general pardon for the murder of Body and for the affray, and the crowd melted away, mollified and in good humour. They had at least got rid of the detested man.

But it turned out that there were exceptions to the 'general' pardon, rather a lot of exceptions, as it transpired. In Launceston alone nine people suffered the revolting death prescribed for the crime of high treason. They were drawn through the town on a hurdle behind a horse; at the gallows they were hanged by the neck, but cut down while still just alive, and thrown to the ground. Then they were disembowelled and their entrails were burnt in front of their still-seeing eyes. Finally, they were beheaded. The mutilated corpses were cut into four quarters, to be displayed wherever the king wished to make a point about the unwisdom of adventuring against the Crown. Nine in Launceston, one more, at least, in Plymouth (a surviving bill records that someone was paid a shilling for the gruesome task of carrying one of the quarters from Plymouth to Tavistock for display) and another in London, where a popular Cornish priest was executed in the usual way. The likelihood is that there were many others, for there were twenty-eight 'exceptions' to the general pardon, and in Tudor times acquittals on this sort of charge were as rare as Plantagenet princes. That all this blood should be spilt for the despised William Body was bad enough, but the rising had been quelled virtually by a trick. Cornwall was seething and ripe for explosion.

On 6 June 1549, three days before the final enforcement of the 'new'

Illustration from an early edition of Foxe's Book of Martyrs. It depicts the sweeping changes that were intended to wipe out all traces of the 'Romish Church' in England.

religious laws, and just three days before the men of Devon rebelled, a great crowd gathered in Bodmin. It is difficult to discover from contemporary sources exactly what had set the whole thing in motion – it was probably another demonstration against the old grievances – but suddenly there was no turning back. The demonstrators were for justice, whatever the cost, and more than willing to shed blood for it.

It quickly became evident that Humphrey Arundell was their leader, though there is confusion as to how precisely this came about. He was thirty-six, an experienced soldier and a member of a distinguished West Country family. At the time he seems to have been in command of a small garrison guarding St Michael's Mount. The account he gave later, in which he said he had been more or less forced into assuming command, hardly rings true when one considers the skilled and resolute leadership he gave

16

the rebels over several months and the intense and sustained loyalty he appears to have inspired.

This time there was to be no dispersal in response to royal promises. Someone shouted 'Castle Kynoch' and they streamed along the narrow lanes and back roads half a mile from Bodmin and took possession of this old fortified place, deserted but serviceable as a temporary headquarters. Then Arundell, with one or two other professional soldiers, various curates and priests, and a few friends, began to set about the unpromising task of establishing military discipline on the enthusiastic rabble.

There was understandable anxiety about the calibre of the leader of the enterprise. Arundell had seen enough of war and insurrection to know that in the early stages of such a campaign the position and influence of those in command, their standing with the ordinary members of the community, and their financial resources were as important as their qualities as soldiers or organizers. There was as yet no indication that the uprising would be anything more than a Cornish effort, and Arundell, looking round at his fellow 'officers' may well have been dismayed. They hardly seemed to be of the stuff to topple the Protector Somerset or the young king.

He himself, though he came from an influential family and had inherited substantial estates in Devon as well as in Cornwall, was neither a nobleman nor very wealthy. This is clearly shown in a list drawn up in 1548 detailing officers and men for the campaign against the French; the modest entry reads: 'Humphrey Arundell and ten on foot'.

In 1549 he did have the Wynslades, John and William – father and son – under his command. They were certainly well off, squires of Tregarrick, well-known gentry in Cornwall and property owners in Devon too, but hardly names to conjure with in London. Then there was John Payne, the Portreeve of St Ives, influential, but only locally; Robert Smyth of Tregonack, young and dashing, with military experience but little else; John Bochym, a minor squire, and his brother Robert, who was in holy orders. There was also Thomas Holmes, long in the service of the Arundell family, one or two other priests and curates, and lastly the Mayor of Bodmin.

No doubt Humphrey Arundell questioned his chances of ultimate success when he looked round the men making camp that day at Castle Kynoch. He probably also recognized the strange family links with rebellion that others would notice in time. He himself and Robert Symth and Wynslade's father-in-law had all served on the grand jury after the killing of William Body, and they had been seen to press for a degree of leniency far from popular in London. Arundell's own maternal grandfather had been involved in the Perkin Warbeck rising against Henry VII (though he had escaped retribution), and John Wynslade's wife Jane was half-sister to William Kendall, who had met a traitor's death for involvement with the Marquis of Exeter's alleged conspiracy eleven years before.

Whatever the truth about the circumstances of Arundell's original involvement with the uprising, once he was embroiled he gave everything he had in terms of leadership and commitment. He saw the urgent necessity for a military success. It would have to be a modest one, but he thought he knew the right target. When he had left St Michael's Mount he had taken with him the small garrison of professional soldiers, but there were a number of residents whose support he knew he could not count on and he had left these behind. Word had reached him that a group of them, hearing of the troubles in Bodmin and wishing to make a conspicuous gesture of loyalty, had taken over the fort and declared their opposition to the infant rebellion. They were now indicating their readiness to defend the Mount.

There was a general enthusiasm in the camp to attack the Mount, but Arundell wisely decided against allowing the blooding of his men at this early stage: the attack had to be a success and with virtually no casualties. His little group of trained soldiers knew every inch of the Mount, so he hand-picked a tiny force and sent them to fight the first engagement of the Western Rebellion.

They waited for low tide and crossed the strip of sand where the causeway now runs. In the main assault each man carried in front of him a great bundle of hay on a fork, which not only made them deceptive targets but absorbed the force of arrows and shot.

The defenders had considered the theory of an attack with equanimity, but found that the reality was a very different matter. They soon panicked and surrendered to Arundell's men. Carew's *Survey of Cornwall* suggests that they surrendered because of a lack of ammunition and food, and because of the fears of the women and children, but in the sixteenth and seventeenth centuries historians found it prudent to write for the winning side. It seems likely that the whole action lasted only an hour, possibly time in which to run out of ammunition but certainly not of food. One notices also that the blame for any lack of stomach for the fight is conveniently attributed to the women and children.

The victorious party returned elated to Castle Kynoch, where some thousands of supporters had by now assembled, including 'many unwilling gentlemen and reluctant knights'. (When the rebels were finally called to account, many of the gentry who had assumed prominent roles pleaded coercion. It is a plea that is hard to swallow, and it was generally ineffective, but it provided the authorities with an excuse to spare a few influential men.) The rebel camp was now so large, and growing daily, that the local authorities felt quite unable to challenge it. It flexed its muscles, drilling its men and hammering out a list of demands, upon the granting of which they would – at least in theory – have all gone home quietly.

Contemporary and near-contemporary accounts, however much they vary in other ways, are constant in suggesting that there were a range of grievances apart from the religious ones. They speak of the rebels' dissatisfaction with recent land reforms, the corruption of the judiciary, and the inadequate protection the law afforded to the common people; yet when the rebels drew up a list of demands to put to the king, they referred only to matters of religion.

This is probably a more important point than many historians have realized. There has been some doubt over the true position of the clergy in the revolt. The rebel priests have been cast in a variety of roles, largely according to the standpoint or faith of the chronicler. Some have painted them as the sole fomenters and instigators, others as reluctant participants, wishing only to protect their poor parishioners. No doubt the truth lies somewhere in between, but it is certain that while Arundell's captains were struggling to knock the fledgling army into shape, the clerics were giving their ecclesiastical grievances a good airing.

Three or four versions of the Articles presented by the rebels to the king have been reported, or deduced from the published answers to them. Foxe's *Acts and Monuments* (1563) is probably the first and certainly the shortest. Here, the eight demands are confined to religious matters. Two later sets of demands, made when the rebels were besieging Exeter, contain fifteen and sixteen requirements respectively, and these longer lists go beyond the religious grievances and into social problems. The original eight articles were written on about 8 June 1549 and sent to London forthwith. They demanded:

1. That baptism should be available on weekdays as well as on Sundays and at any time of need.
2. That bishops should carry out confirmation on request.
3. That mass be celebrated without any communication between the priest and any other member of the congregation, as in the days when the transubstantiation of Christ was formally and fully accepted as fact.
4. That the host be reserved in churches as before.
5. That worshippers should have holy bread and holy water.
6. That the service should be sung and said in the choir, and not set out 'like a Christmas play'.
7. That priests should not marry.
8. That the Six Articles set out by Henry VIII should continue in force until the present king attained the age of royal competence (twenty-four).

Arundell's men had to wait some time for the king's answer, and when it arrived it did not satisfy them. It was accompanied by the offer of a pardon for anyone who laid down his weapons and returned home, but the rebels remembered the pardon offered after the killing of William Body, and took no notice. It became clear to those who were organizing the camp and were responsible for the morale of the insurgents that they had spent long enough in camp. They needed to move to where they might live off the land more successfully and with less inconvenience to the local people. Thus the great march got under way.

Later, during the trial of the rebel leaders, Arundell's force at the start of the march up-country was described as being three thousand strong, 'With banners unfurled, swords, shields, clubs, cannon, halberds, lances and other arms both offensive and defensive, armed and in war-like manner'. While this account may have exaggerated their martial appearance, to make an effect in court, the rebels certainly meant to march on the capital and show the king's uncle, the Lord Protector, what they thought of him. Morale was high in the early days, sustained by the steady stream of recruits, and they really thought that the rest of the country would rise with them to turn out an almost universally unpopular regime. Like every marching group, the Cornishmen developed a sense of comradeship and purpose, and there would have been cheering and encouragement enough as they walked across the wastes of Bodmin Moor, bleak even in summer. The 1549 rebellion was launched, and there was no going back.

As soon as they crossed the Tamar into Devon a large part of the company was detached and sent towards Plymouth to see if that city would respond to their cause, and to attempt to rally further support in the area. Surviving documents do not tell us who commanded this important branch of the army, but it would be surprising if Robert Smyth were not amongst its leaders, both because of his military record and because it was his area, which would have made him well placed to appeal for the support of the local gentry.

They arranged to meet a week or two later, whatever happened, in Crediton. This was felt to be the right place to regroup and make plans about Exeter. They wanted to take Plymouth if they could, but were clearly prepared to bypass the city if it put up determined resistance. They had to balance speed of advance, and the consequent shortage of time for recruiting, against the extra time any delay would give the government to react against them.

Just before or just after they divided their forces, the rebels were confronted by a band of loyalists under the command of Sir Richard Grenville, whose stronghold, Trematon Castle, was near by. Grenville had been the head of the Commission that had tried those accused of killing William Body the year before; there was probably little love lost between him and Arundell. When Sir Richard saw the strength of the rebel army he took refuge in Trematon and organized a defence. But his supporters had either little stomach for the contest, or too much sympathy for the rebels, and deserted by night. Trematon was soon taken, and, according to Carew's *Survey of Cornwall*, Grenville himself was imprisoned in Launceston Gaol.

In the event, Plymouth yielded almost at once, though its castle held out, and most of the rebel force quickly turned north, for Tavistock and Crediton.

In her excellent account, *The Western Rebellion of 1549*, Frances Rose-Troup, bereft for once of contemporary sources, conjures up straggling columns swarming across the wilds of Dartmoor. It is quite true that the shortest line from Tavistock to Crediton lies over the moor, but to go round the western and northern edge by way of Lydford and Okehampton takes very little longer and is much easier and safer going. Certainly some of the insurgents chose this lowland route and thus virtually stumbled on the support that, unknown to them, was brewing in a sleepy Devon village that Whit Sunday.

—*4*—

Trouble at Sampford Courtenay

A few miles west of Crediton, just off the northern edge of Dartmoor, lies one of the prettiest villages in all Devonshire. A sleepy, charming place of cob and thatch and mellow stone, ablaze with flowers in the summer, Sampford Courtenay has changed little since the Middle Ages.

On your left as you enter the church is a tiny door. Behind this is a narrow stone spiral staircase which leads to the roof of the south aisle. From there you have a perfect view of the little churchyard, and the gravestones leaning with the weight of the centuries. On one side the warm and peaceful churchyard is bounded by the inner wall of the Church House and the whole area seems tailored to fit sweetly round the church itself. From your high vantage point you can drink in the tranquillity of the place and may well be misled into thinking that nothing of consequence, and certainly nothing violent, could ever have tainted it.

Yet here the spark was struck that so nearly changed the course of our history. Here the Devon rising flared up and joined the Cornishmen's revolt. Without the Devon contingent, which doubled their strength, Arundell's men numbered three or possibly four thousand. On their own it is highly doubtful that they could have laid siege to Exeter. They would very probably have been brought to battle within weeks and destroyed by the king's army that was now waiting irresolutely in East Devon to face them.

As Whit Sunday 1549 approached, almost the sole topics of conversation in Sampford Courtenay were the new laws, the new prayer-book, and whether Father Harper really would abandon his vestments and use the new form of service, in obedience to instructions. News of the Cornishmen's progress arrived at the village daily, no doubt embellished with a fair amount of exaggeration. Some kind of showdown was

Sampford Courtenay Church

confidently expected. The local magistrates, aware of Father Harper's strong loyalty to the old ways, would have made it clear to him that from 9 June the law of the land would require his compliance. Father Harper knew that the magistrates themselves would be at church on Whit Sunday; indeed, he knew exactly which of the boxed pews they would be in.

On the Sunday the village was unusually crowded. The religious festival had attracted many families from the outlying farms, hundreds more had travelled in to see or be part of the trouble they sensed was coming, and, in addition, the day after Whit Sunday was the occasion of the very popular annual ale festival. For days the roads and tracks from Exbourne, Jacobstowe, Honeychurch, Sampford Chapel, North Tawton and even Sticklepath had been full, with donkeys, fortune-tellers, farm labourers and their families making a weekend of it, travelling friars, hawkers scenting a fat profit, and all the curious or angry populace coming to see for themselves just what would happen.

Sampford Courtenay church is of a good size but there were no empty pews that morning. It was packed, and buzzing with speculation. When the priest entered the chancel the congregation must have been stunned. He had left off his old vestments after all, he did use the English version of the prayer-book and he abided by the new order of service laid down by law. Hardly anyone had imagined he would.

Reverence for God's house kept the rising tide of uproar under control until the service ended, but as the church emptied the complaints were loud and the acrimony sustained. The people felt robbed, both by the loss of their rituals and regalia and by the fact that their priest, whom everyone had expected to make a gesture of defiance at least, seemed to have caved in without even a token protest. In the road outside agitators made speeches on behalf of the Cornish rebels, and these were very well received. The devout countrymen were very conscious that it was the Sabbath, however. Eventually, after shouting their solidarity and affirming their determination to meet there the following day, the crowd dispersed and an uneasy peace lay over Sampford Courtenay.

The first direct action of the Devon rising was the work of the common people. On the Monday, the crowd outside the church was larger and angrier than it had been the day before, though few of them would have dared accost the rector when he arrived. Yet two did; Thomas Underhill, a tailor, and William Segar, a labourer, barred the priest's way and demanded to know his intentions for the day's service.

Most people knew that Father Harper privately supported the old faith. He had little love for the old king, and indeed had held the position of Clerk to the Closet in the service of Catherine Parr, last wife of Henry VIII, and was still in her service after the king died. He was known to be a supporter and confidant of Mary Tudor and there are records of complaints to the Princess Mary that her 'chaplain' in the West Country had been brewing up trouble and dissent. On this occasion, however, Harper was playing very safe, perhaps waiting to be coerced, for he apparently told Segar and Underhill that he must do as the law stipulated and say the new service in the common tongue. Incensed, the two men harangued him until he agreed to say the old-style mass that day.

The Exeter Guildhall Manuscript of Hoker* comments: 'Whether it were with his will or against his will he replied to their minds and yielded to their wills and forthwith ravessheth [clothed] himself in his old Popish attire and sayeth mass and all such services as in times past accustomed.'

Being treated to the old-style service they loved does not seem to have pacified the crowd, but to have reinforced their determination to resist the new. Besides, the law had now been broken and the magistrates were sure to hear of it soon enough. The people were almost relieved that the die had been cast. The speeches became more impassioned and there was much talk of the approaching Cornishmen.

News travels fast. Four Justices of the Peace quickly set off for the village. The escort they had collected seemed adequate to them, for they were not accustomed to much trouble from their own people. Hoker gives the names of the four who came (he has been widely quoted by subsequent writers): Alexander Wood of Ashridge, North Tawton; Sir Hugh Pollard of King's Nympton; Anthony Harvey of Columb John; and a fourth, Mark Slader of Bath. It has tended to be accepted that they were all local Justices, but no magistrate from as far away as Bath could have functioned in the Okehampton area. When we discover that Mark Slader was Alexander Wood's son-in-law, it seems highly probable that he was visiting his wife's father at the time and, being himself a magistrate in his own area, came along to support the older man.

Hearing that the Justices of the King's Peace were close, the ringleaders conferred. No doubt they were emboldened by the numbers and the vociferousness of their supporters. The rebel leaders decided to refuse to parley with the Justices unless they were prepared to leave their escort and come alone into a nearby field to discuss matters.

The magistrates were unsure what to do. Official accounts indicate that they could have been more resolute and even that they had enough men to

---

*The historian John Hoker, or Hooker, alias John Vowell, was Chamberlain to the Mayor of Exeter, and witnessed the siege of the city. (*See* Bibliography.)

take military action if they chose. However, it seems highly probable that the four gentlemen were appalled both by the size of the crowd and by the strength of feeling that was being displayed. At all events they settled for discretion and agreed to meet the leaders of the mob without the benefit of their bodyguard. Hoker is, as usual, quite convinced where the blame lay:

> There having had conference a pretty while together did in the end depart without anything done at all whereof as there redounded some weakness in the said Justices which were so white livered as they would not or durst not to repress the rages of the people, so thereof ensued such a scab as passed their cure and such a fire as they were not able to quench: for the commoners having now their wills were set upon a pin that the game was theirs and they had won the garland before they had run the race.

By this time Sampford Courtenay Church House had become the rebels' headquarters, and here it was that they took their first prisoner. William Hellyons was by all accounts an amiable and respected man; he was certainly a brave one. He was most likely a yeoman of some substance, and, though accounts differ, a long-time resident of the district. On this occasion, however, he was the wrong man speaking at the wrong time. Courageously but unwisely, he upbraided the rebels for breaking the law and urged them to go home peaceably. By this time the magistrates had gone, but when brought to the Church House headquarters, Hellyons would not moderate his tone of reproof. Seeing that his words were having no effect, he turned contemptuously to leave. No one stopped him, though several angrily followed him out to the stone steps leading down to the street below.

Suddenly there was the flash of a hedger's billhook and Hellyons was on his knees, awash in his own blood. He was speedily hacked to death. In one edition of his *History of Exeter* Jenkins names the attacker as one 'Githbridge', and, in another, 'Lithibridge'. Other sources give 'Lethbridge', which is a common local name. Jenkins records that once Lethbridge had felled Hellyons with a blow to the neck; '... notwithstanding his pitiful requests and lamentations, a number of the rest fell upon him and slew him and cut him into small pieces', which does not accord with the popularity he was supposed to have enjoyed in the area.

There is no evidence of remorse at the first spilling of blood in the county (in view of how the rebellion spread, this is hardly surprising). Indeed, it seems that the deed was applauded and that being the first to act, at a time when a repressed wish for action was widespread in the district, gave the Sampford men a position of eminence.

Sampford Courtenay Church House

Interestingly, it appears that Father Harper organized a swift burial to tidy up the affair, but, as Rose-Troup records, he nevertheless insisted that Hellyons be buried 'with the body laid North and South, to indicate that the deceased was an outcast from the Church, a heretic'.

This was a strangely unforgiving action, especially when one considers the manner of Hellyons' death. Father Harper may have been punishing him for advocating the new law and the new religion. Other reports describing Hellyons as a Fleming by origin may also shed light on the priest's motives. If Hellyons were Flemish, it may be that, in Father Harper's opinion, he had never embraced the true faith. There is another possible explanation. The men who slaughtered Hellyons were devout believers – otherwise they would not have become involved in this dangerous business – and the priest may have felt that by burying the victim as a heretic he had made a gesture of absolution to the killers and reaffirmed the rightness of their cause, as though they were fighting a religious war. He may have used the incident to harden the rebels' resolve and allay some of the regrets, doubts or guilt that might weaken their determination.

With the slaying of Hellyons and the defiant celebration of the old-style mass the Sampford men had burned all their boats, but things were happening too swiftly, and the excitement was too great, for anyone to worry about it at the time. It was rumoured that Humphrey Arundell was already at Yewton Arundell, his estate near Crediton, and had started to train volunteers; many Devonians were said to be hurrying to join him.

On the morning of 11 June there came cheering at the other end of Sampford Courtenay, down by the New Inn (then only ten years old), and people began shouting that the Cornishmen had arrived. The crowd would have left the wide road in front of the church and rushed to meet them. The cheering tin miners, some of whom had crossed Dartmoor, while others had skirted it, were carrying bundles of provisions and a great variety of home-made and other weapons as they toiled up the road. Swept along by the tide of enthusiastic comradeship, the men of Sampford Courtenay – some without making any proper arrangements with their families – ran to join them on that crowded, dusty road to the East.

Some writers have wondered at the slowness of the government's response to the Western risings. Why was firm action not taken before matters became so serious? The remoteness of the area and the difficulties of communication have been put forward as reasons, but these are easy to exaggerate.

By the standards of the day, the government had a good information service, though they did not always take the information they received as seriously as they should. The people of Devon and Cornwall were looked upon as primitive, backward and docile, and although the Duke of Somerset was sent despatches from the far West several times a week, he was slow to realize the gravity of the situation.

Communications by road were also pretty good. There were normally thirteen staging posts between Plymouth and London, and eleven between Exeter and the capital. Even when travelling with one's whole family, with luggage in carts, the journey could be completed in four days. By riding at a gallop and changing horses at each stage, a horseman could make the journey in not much over thirty-six hours, providing he had the stamina and could afford good mounts, which would be the case for someone on the king's business.

Apart from a degree of misjudgement of the situation, there was a more fundamental reason for the government's delayed response to the risings: the Privy Council did not know what to do and hoped to get away with doing nothing. In other parts of the country their inaction had paid off and revolts had fizzled out. The Crown was desperately short of money; its resources were severely strained, its credit poor. And there were always other apparently more pressing and important matters to be attended to.

England was in the middle of a war with Scotland, there was a threat of trouble with the French, the economy was at a low ebb, the people were deeply disturbed by recent land-reform measures and there was division and dissension among the king's advisers themselves. During the summer of 1549 there were actual or rumoured risings in Hertfordshire, Somerset, Gloucester, Worcester, Wiltshire, Hampshire, Sussex, Essex, Kent, Yorkshire, Rutland and Norfolk, so that when a sweat-stained messenger staggered in with news of the Cornish rebellion the hearts of the Council must have sunk. Only two days later came a harassed despatch from the Devon Justices describing their failure to contain the Sampford Courtenay affray and their fears that the Devonshire men were now up in arms with their Cornish cousins. It may have been on the very same day that the Council received the first accounts of serious rioting in Oxfordshire and further troubles in Berkshire. The sheer difficulty of establishing priorities, with very limited resources, added to the concern to maintain some flexibility of military response in the future, inclined the authorities towards delay.

It was becoming clear, however, that the government needed to act swiftly, though even now they hoped to do so with the minimum of expense. There were not enough troops under arms that could readily be spared, and the hope was that military force might not be needed. What they wanted was a trouble-shooter, a man with good knowledge of and influence in the West Country, a man who was shrewd and persuasive, but also had military experience, in case it came to battle. As yet little blood had been spilt; there might still be time to appear reasonable and conciliatory, and by acting with generosity appease the people and persuade them to go home in peace. They needed a special man.

The Duke of Somerset (or one of his aides) had a better idea: use two men. The two Carews fitted the bill perfectly. Sir Gawen was in London and could be ready at a moment's notice, and while it was true that his nephew, Sir Peter, was in Lincolnshire, he could quickly be recalled to the capital. It is perhaps an indication of Sir Peter's public spirit that, although he was actually on his honeymoon when summoned from Lincolnshire, within five days he was galloping along the Great West Road from London with his uncle. The journey gave the two knights a chance to reflect on the very difficult mission they had acquired.

The Carews were no fools. They had experience of court affairs and understood politics and pragmatism, but they were soldiers by training and in this enterprise they rode for the king without the forces they would need to effect a military solution. Some troops would be made available to them at Exeter, but not many. This worried the Carews, but the words of the Protector, ringing in their ears, worried them even more. Leniency, he had repeatedly told them, would be the key to success in this venture. He had admitted that they would be dealing with out-and-out rebels who no doubt richly deserved hanging – and worse – but force had to be the last resort. Furthermore, it might take weeks to prepare the means to exert force; the government would not sanction this unless the need proved desperate. The people must be persuaded by gentle means. The Carews knew their West Countrymen, especially the people of Devon, for their family home, Mohun's Ottery, was near Honiton. They also knew, and this must have worried them, that, while normally placid and slow to anger, Devonians were nevertheless fiercely stubborn and steadfastly brave when taking part in what they saw as a just and noble cause.

The Carews carried in their saddle-bags a message from the Duke of Somerset for the gentlemen of Devon. The document had been signed by the young king, but it was clearly the Duke of Somerset who had drafted it. The letter said that the king would accept that the common people had been led astray and that he would pardon them if they went home peaceably. The gentry were to explain this to the people as best they could. However, after this act of leniency, any who continued to rebel would be proceeded against with the full weight of the law.

Saddle sore but driven by the urgency of their mission, the Carews hurried westwards, changing their exhausted horses at each staging post and snatching a hurried meal where they could. Gentlemen did not normally travel with such haste, but these were not normal times and any delay might prove damaging to the king's cause. When at last they clattered wearily through Exeter's North Gate and dismounted at the Guildhall, they sent at once for the mayor, the sheriffs and the magistrates.

News of an alarming nature had just come in. A great number of commoners, led by some gentlemen, were occupying the town of Crediton. Worse still, it was confirmed that this was indeed a joint force of Cornish rebels and Sampford men, and that Devonians were flocking hourly to their banner.

—5—

Crediton,
and the
Burning of the Barns

The Carews must have made very fast time on the road from London. Rose-Troup (who had access to more sources on this subject than anyone else, before or since) is emphatic that the two knights arrived in Exeter on 21 June and, in spite of their exhaustion, left for Crediton on the same day. However, the king had dated the memorandum they carried 20 June, and the document still exists to prove this. The Carews must have left Richmond at dawn on the 20th, having probably spent the previous night there. The king would have entrusted the document to them on the evening of the 19th, giving it the date of their departure in order to impress the urgency of the matter on those for whom the letter was intended. That way, riding post, Sir Gawen and Sir Peter could have arrived at Exeter in the afternoon of the 21st.

They must have been bone weary after riding nearly two hundred miles, with eleven changes of horses. It would have made sense to settle for an early night at The Mermaid, the Exeter tavern used by the most important visitors of the time, and set off refreshed for Crediton the following day. The situation could not have been dealt with any better that day than the next, but impetuosity was a Carew failing, just as conscientiousness was a Carew virtue, and these two characteristics dragged the weary warriors the extra seven miles to see for themselves whether things were indeed as black as they had been painted. This followed upon a conference with the 'chief men of the county' at which it had been decided that the Carews had no alternative but to make a start on their mission.

Subsequent recriminations make it clear that the Carews had spoken in rather over-confident terms about their rapport with the good peasantry of Devon and their ability to handle them. One can picture the scene, and almost sympathize with the Carews. They had, after all, managed their tenants successfully, and they had certainly been respected and liked in the Honiton area. They did know their people and in anything like normal circumstances would prove this again.

The rashness lay in boasting about it in advance, and at the wrong time. The fact was that they had never encountered the men of Devon in this mood. However, none of this was as yet evident to Sir Peter or his uncle, Sir Gawen, as they trotted over the bridge approaching the Exeter end of Crediton. They had been told that the little town was defended but they were not prepared for what they met.

The earliest version of the Hoker Manuscript – the basic source material since Hoker was himself in Exeter at the time – is in the Bodleian Library at Oxford. It contains some graphic details. Because of an indecipherable portion, the following extract is a combination of the Bodleian and the Guildhall versions. The first part is taken from the Guildhall version, which is probably the later of the two.

> By some secret intelligence advertised of the coming of the gentlemen towards them and they fully resolved not to yield one iote from their determinations but to maintain their cause taken in hand, and to this end do arme and make themselves strong with such armour and furniture as they had. ...
>
> ... they entrenched and rampired* the high way at the town's end leading towards Exeter and had hanged up great plough chains uppon them and had fortified the same with men and munition.

There were at that time two large barns, built no doubt of cob and thatch, which crowded close to the Exeter road and stood solidly on each side of it. It was between these that the people of Crediton had fixed the heavy plough chains. The walls of these same barns were apparently those pierced for the sniping positions. Maclean's biography of Sir Peter Carew describes it thus: 'On either side of the road from Exeter and adjoining the entrenchments were two barns; the walls of these they pierced with loops and holes for their shot, and complenished them with men well appointed with bows and arrows and other weapons to prevent entrance to the town.'

The Carews had taken the precaution of sending a screen of scouts out on the road ahead. When they crossed the river and began the left-handed

---

*When the verb 'to rampire' is used as Hoker uses it, it normally means to throw up an earth defence, a bank and a ditch, though occasionally the word is used when speaking of barricading with fallen trees. As a noun it obviously refers to the defence that has been made. It is a pity that such a fine-sounding word should have fallen into disuse.

curve towards the town they were waved down by their own advance party and warned that the road was solidly blocked and fortified against them. After some discussion and no doubt a good deal of peering over hedges and questioning the commander of the advance party, the decision was made to advance on foot, both to facilitate taking immediate cover if necessary and because it would give a less warlike look to the expedition and make it easier, perhaps, to start a discussion with the rebels.

It took the Carews a long time to live down the humiliation of this encounter. The Duke of Somerset had impressed on them the need to talk, consult, persuade, and this they planned to do – if they were given the chance. At the head of his now dismounted force Sir Peter strode boldly towards the barricade, shouted out who he was and made it known that he wished to parley with the leaders of the opposition. He had no information about the precise numbers of rebels encamped there, but the high level of manning at the barricade looked somewhat ominous. Sir Peter and Sir Gawen shouted again, becoming conscious that they were in danger of looking foolish. At this point something enraged them, though we cannot be sure exactly what; perhaps a jeering comment or an arrow past the ear. When for the third time they attempted to make contact, they were informed that nobody was going to talk to them and advised, for the sake of their health, to go back to whomever had sent them. Even as they returned to speak to their men in the shelter of the ditch, the Carews had clearly decided to attack.

It was evident to the others that the Carews were shaking with rage. Sir Peter's pride had been badly hurt. His vaunted ability to handle the Devon peasant was rebounding on him and he was desperate to retrieve matters militarily and teach these countrymen a lesson. As Froude points out in his *History of England*, Sir Peter had been used to a somewhat higher calibre of opponent in the wars with the French and he refused to let a pack of village churls get the better of him.

The consultation in the ditch resulted in a decision to make a swift and decisive assault and teach the rebels some manners. Sir Peter was forced to admit that he did not really have enough men for the task he was now setting them, but they were trained men and the difference in quality would surely tip the balance against the difference in numbers.

A soldier of Sir Peter's experience ought not to have made this mistake. He had had a good chance to assess the strength of the defensive position, and he should have known better than to make such a decision while his judgement was clouded by anger, as it certainly was. The small force made a determined attack; the men were bravely led, but it was obvious within moments that they had misjudged the enemy's fire-power. The response from the fortified barns was brisk and well directed. There were clearly some real soldiers in there somewhere and the rampire was stoutly defended. Suddenly the attackers found themselves running in disarray, leaving a score or more of dead or wounded behind them. The ironic jeers of the defenders came from the barns, quite literally adding insult to injury. Then followed an extraordinary incident, puzzling in its effect and in the highly unpredictable consequences that followed in its wake.

Sir Hugh Pollard had been one of the original Justices who had hurried to Sampford Courtenay to see what could be done about the Whit Sunday affray, but he was not among those who had ridden to Crediton with the Carews. Instead he had sent a posse of his men and one or two family retainers from the house at King's Nympton. One of these, called Foxe, had what he thought was a brilliant idea, one that indeed ought to have had good rather than disastrous consequences. In the ill-fated attempt to storm the rampire he had noticed that either the hay harvest had been early, or the previous year's crop had been unusually heavy, for both the barns were substantially stocked with hay and straw and could easily be set alight. This, without telling anybody, he promptly did. The strong breeze fanned the flames so that they were soon roaring out of control.

Panic swept through the defenders to a surprising degree, and they ran back out of the barns, out of the fortified rampires and indeed out of the town, presumably because, with the barns gone, they had no other fortified position. When the barns were finally burnt out and the attackers cautiously advanced, expecting every minute to be fired upon, they were met by stillness and silence. They pushed on into the town, and found it undefended and largely deserted. The Carews did not know what to do. The rebels had certainly fled Crediton, but the kings's men did not have a large enough force to hold the town against an enemy which was sure to be all around them. The Carews had achieved none of their aims, and there was no one with whom they could now parley or treat.

All in all they had no alternative but to return to Exeter, and could hardly be thought to be returning victorious. The only casualties had been on their side, and they could not boast of passing on Somerset's message to the rebels as there had been no one prepared to listen to them at the beginning and no one present to do so at the end. Sir Peter sat down that evening and wrote his report, which dealt with the need for more men rather than with the details of what had happened.

A quite unexpected result of the firing of the Crediton barns was the effect on the people in the countryside as a whole. Looked at objectively, it was an obvious and acceptable military action to reduce a fortified place that could not otherwise, at that time, be stormed or taken. Although one of the men had actually done it on his own initiative, it might reasonably have been ordered by the commander. What happened, however, was that the burning of the barns became a byword throughout the South West for the unscrupulous and unfair methods of the king's men.

The Carews were, frankly, rather unlucky in this. The rebels had a degree of leadership from soldiers of good family, but they capitalized on the Crediton affair, in terms of propaganda value, through their intellectual backers, the dissident priests. They not only saw the way to make the most of the event, but they had the means of doing so: parish pulpits. It was easy to convince country people that those who were prepared to set fire to other people's livelihood were not only wicked but unsporting. The firing of the barns grew in the telling into a much bigger thing than it actually was. Feeling was drummed up cleverly, and, in the circumstances, quite reasonably, since this was above all a battle for the hearts and minds of country people. In any event, the resolve of the insurgents was greatly hardened, their support throughout the South West increased, and hundreds of extra recruits came to Arundell's banner.

A contemporary account of the propaganda effects of the Carews' indifferent piece of public relations work is tinged with anger at the injustice of the events as the writer saw them:

> The noise of this fire and burning was in post haste and as it were in a moment carried and blasted throughout the whole country and the Common people upon false reports and, of a gnat making an elephant, noised and spread it abroad that the gentlemen were altogether bent to over-run, spoil and destroy them: and in this rage as it were a swarm of wasps they cluster themselves in great troops and multitudes, some in one place and some in another fortifying and entrenching themselves as though the enemy were ready to invade and assail them.

Very soon after this there was an incident that illustrates the dramatic change in attitude of the surrounding villages. It is very fully recorded by Hoker since it involved the father of a man he knew well, later to become very famous, Sir Walter Raleigh. It seems that Mr Raleigh senior was travelling on horseback from his East Devon home to Exeter. Passing through the village of Clyst St Mary he noticed an old woman going to church clutching her beads and her prayer-book. Although it was scarcely his business he took it upon himself to dismount, stop the old woman and read her a lecture on the new religion and her duty to uphold the law and abandon her present superstitious beliefs. Naturally incensed by this, she hurried into the church and told the congregation about the strange gentleman who had so affronted her.

According to Hoker's version of events the woman greatly exaggerated any threats Raleigh may have made. She reported that he had said that unless they forswore holy water and other rites the gentry could be relied on to come from Exeter to burn them out just as they had done at Crediton. One cannot tell how Hoker knew exactly what happened in the church, though he may have been able to piece together reports from other people who were there. He was not the kind of historian to be deterred from producing a piece with a flavour suggesting an eye-witness account. In this case he manages, as usual, to lend credibility to what is almost certainly a heavily biased account. Here is an extract:

> ... saying that she was threatened by the gentleman, that except she should leave her beads and give over holy bread and holy water the gentlemen would burn them out of their houses and spoil them, with many other speeches very false and untrue and whereof no talk at all had passed between the gentleman and her: notwithstanding she had not so soon spoken but that she was believed: and in all haste, like a sort of wasps flying out of the church and gat them to the town which is not far from thence and there began to entrench and fortify the town, sending abroad into the country round about the news aforesaid of their doings in hand: flocking and procuring as many as they could to come and join with them ....

Apart from all this, it is beyond doubt that the congregation were so annoyed with Mr Raleigh that they chased after him and caught him before he got to the gates of the county town and might well have done him some considerable mischief, had he not been rescued by some sailors from Exmouth, possibly employees of his, who saved him from the furious people.

On Saturday 22 June, the day after the expedition to Crediton, there was a conference in Exeter, at which the Carews clearly had a none too happy time. A number of people asked how, in view of the Carews' previous confidence about handling Devonians, things could have gone so wrong. At one stage Sir Peter was stung to round on the Justices and point out that Clyst St Mary, just outside the city's gates, was now fortified, and he implied criticism of them for allowing this to happen so close to home. He also told them of the incident with Mr Raleigh as an example of the ugly temper of the people they were supposed to keep peaceable.

The expedition to Crediton, while certainly producing spectacular results, could hardly have been described as successful, but it was decided that the same kind of essay must be made again; to be fair, it is hard to see what else they could have tried. The Carews were to head another

36

expedition to find out for themselves what was happening at Clyst St Mary. This time Sir Thomas Denys and Sir Hugh Pollard, who had not gone in person to Crediton, were to be of the party. Perhaps they insisted on being included so that they could see at first hand what was going wrong; perhaps the Carews pressed them to be there since they had been critical of the handling of the earlier task force. They planned to leave at first light the next day, which was a Sunday.

At dawn, therefore, on 23 June, a column clattered along Southgate Street, with the cathedral to their left, and headed out on the Topsham road. Dawns comes very early at midsummer and no doubt many of them were only half awake when they gathered in the courtyard of The Mermaid, a rendezvous chosen for the convenience of the Carews, who were staying at the inn. When they reached what is now the Countess Wear roundabout they would have reined their horses' heads to the left, skirting the site of the modern golf-course and heading for the little bridge over the Clyst.

Some historians have described the surprise of the party as they approached the bridge to find another rampire blocking their path. It is unlikely that they were surprised. They had already received reports of such fortifications, and Raleigh had stressed the pervading atmosphere of tension when he had reported to them his own close-run escape.

As before, Sir Peter dismounted and went forward on foot towards the rebel position to try to speak to their leaders. He had a narrow escape at this point for he seems to have overlooked the fact that he was becoming both well known and well hated in the rebel ranks. Was he not the monster, as they told it, who had burned the Crediton barns? Did not his men have similar plans to smoke out and despoil poor men throughout the county who were standing up for what their forefathers had held sacred?

On the Clyst rampire, one John Hammon – or Hammond – from nearby Woodbury, a gun-layer now, though a blacksmith by calling, was at that moment calmly preparing to despatch Sir Peter into eternity. He had set his sights and was in the very act of firing his piece when another man, named as Hugh Osborne and in the service of Serjeant Prydeox, stopped him from putting flame to the touch-powder. Sir Peter seems to have remained in ignorance of how close he had come to oblivion.

Nonetheless, the Carews' way was still barred. They shouted out that they came in peace. At least, that was the intention but the choice of words was unfortunate. As reported, though not as far as I can discover by anyone actually present, they wished 'to advertise them that we were come to talk friendly with them, and also to satisfy them if they had any cause of grief or were by anybody misused'.

The rebels were outraged. They felt that such words must betoken treachery. Of *course* they felt misused, that is why they were literally up in arms. If they had not felt misused would half the county be in a state of revolt? The gentlemen had either not taken their action seriously or were planning some devious move. The leaders took their time. They decided that they would not allow Sir Peter in but were prepared to receive a deputation as long as no armed escort accompanied it. They knew and, to a degree, trusted Sir Thomas Denys, who lived in the next village. They said they would talk to him, and to Sir Hugh Pollard and Thomas Yarde if those three would come in alone, and providing the gentlemen outside the village gave their word that no harm would come to the villagers.

So the three went in, leaving the Carews to twiddle their thumbs outside and brood over the fact that they were being excluded from events of which they were supposed to be in charge. Denys, Yarde and Pollard were inside a long time – all day, in fact – and towards nightfall those waiting outside began to wonder if they had been butchered. Some began talking about starting an attack, but others urged them to caution in case precipitate action should bring reprisals on their friends within.

A few of the hotter-headed horsemen could no longer be content with their passive role. Thinking to explore the possibilities of a future attack to rescue their friends, they went and probed with lances and staves to discover the depth of the water and the mud in the tidal river; they might need a ford if the bridge was too heavily defended. The villagers saw what they were doing, and were enraged. The situation was very unstable for a time and mistrust was rife.

Well after sunset the three men came safely out and returned over the bridge, but with little to show for a hard day's bargaining except a bad temper. It irked them to have done as badly as Sir Peter in persuading their fellow countrymen of a prudent course of action. They all trooped rather mournfully back to The Mermaid, where dinner had been arranged for the magistrates, civic dignitaries and negotiators. On the road back to Exeter Sir Peter repeatedly pressed for news of what had passed but was told very little.

That evening an ugly scene developed, and after dinner there was a good deal of recrimination and ill humour. Sir Thomas Denys and Sir Hugh Pollard defended their attempts at negotiation and wondered pointedly if Sir Peter would have done any better, considering his record at Crediton. The row lasted some time, and was heard by the servants and reported in due course to the rebel leaders, who were very interested to hear that the gentry were far from united in their own cause.

These reports must have emboldened the rebels, for the next day they virtually laid siege to the city. Seeing that a siege was now inevitable, the mayor urged some of the people to go back to their own estates as the city did not have enough food put by for extra mouths. Although the siege would not actually begin for another eight days, the rebels already controlled most of the surrounding countryside. On 24 June the Carews and their party left the city for their own homes, and Sir Peter set off for London. Many of them were held up and captured, for most of the country lanes were blocked. Those captured (Walter Raleigh among them) were kept in the tower of St Sidwell's Church, outside the city walls, for many weeks.

Sir Peter dodged the road-blocks and rode post-haste for London. In view of what he had to report it cannot have been a comfortable journey for him.

$$-6-$$

London Reacts

London's reactions to the traumatic events unfolding themselves in the West have often seemed hard to understand. Why did the Lord Protector, the young king's uncle and the single most powerful man in the country, act as he did? Was the Regent a weak man? Did the government have any idea how serious events were becoming? Any answers to these questions that seem concise and positive are almost certainly wrong. Most historians have been content to label the Duke of Somerset a liberal, but it is more complex than that. His character was full of conflicting strands and history has dealt unkindly with him in some ways. G. M. Trevelyan has described him as: '... a strange mixture of pride and humility, selfishness and pure public spirit. He was more honest, humane and democratic in spirit than other politicians of the time'.

He was certainly guilty of grabbing for himself a share of any spoils that were available. After the dissolution of the monasteries, the chantries and guilds were the next institutions to be plundered. The original Somerset House, a palace in all but name, he built from his own lavish share from this spoliation. He was also very interested in personal power and aimed unwisely high for himself. Wolsey, of course, had managed to acquire power, and retain it for quite a long time, but he had had the support of a mature, vigorous and unscrupulous king to whom he had made himself indispensable. This kind of insurance Somerset lacked, and it is largely for this reason that the Prayer-Book Rebellion claimed him as a victim when the time of reckoning arrived.

In many ways he was too complicated a man. On occasions when he should have gone ahead single-mindedly his scruples often tripped him up. His inclinations were towards liberalism and tolerance, but he tried to exercise them at inappropriate times. In Parliament he introduced a

The Lord Protector

number of reforms of a relatively progressive nature, he did not persecute either Protestants or Catholics for religious beliefs unless they broke the law, and he steered through the repeal of several of Henry VIII's most oppressive statutes. He encouraged the free discussion of religious beliefs when the country was nowhere near ready for such a step, and he was sometimes too conciliatory when he should have been firm. As a result there was, after him, a swing back to a much more repressive regime than would have been necessary or acceptable if he had held the reins more decisively himself.

When it came to planning, the contradictions in his character led him to be long-winded, over-cautious and reluctant to delegate, and he would write out in interminable detail every possible course of action that might be taken in response to every conceivable turn of events. He thus tried to bind his subordinates into lines of action predetermined by himself when he ought to have trusted them to use their own discretion and initiative.

He had a streak of considerable stinginess that contrasted unpleasantly with his capacity to indulge himself, and was eager to get things, for himself and for his government, on the cheap. One must remember, however, that he found himself in extraordinary difficulties with the Exchequer empty, wars on two fronts, the currency debased and royal credit strained, to say the least. Sometimes he was mean simply because there were no resources at his disposal to be anything else. By the standards of his time he was not a bad man, nor even a weak one, though he did tend to vacillate when the different strands in his make-up conflicted, which quite often they did. He also tended at times to pomposity and did not seem to have the trick of arousing public sympathy or popularity.

One thing which had seemed likely to improve Somerset's standing with ordinary men and women was his recent development into a credible and successful general. In the Scottish wars he had built up a good reputation as a commander, and many people hoped he would himself take control of an army and deal promptly with the insurrection in the South West. Subsequent events, especially the eventual defection of the man he did choose for the task, no doubt made him wish he had taken command himself, but at the time the rebellion seemed to be happening a long way away. He may have felt that, with so many other areas in active or potential revolt, he must himself remain near the centre of the national scene. He also doubtless underestimated the gravity of the Western Rebellion.

In London, although the gravity of the situation was not fully understood, some preparations were being made to assemble a force even before Sir Peter Carew staggered in after his long ride from Exeter towards the end of June. The news he brought cheered nobody.

Now came pressure on Somerset to be more ruthless and to act as the late King Harry would have acted. Some of the letters of advice he received of which records remain are very surprising and scarcely conceal their writers' obvious opinion that the Lord Protector was too weak for the job. A well-known example is the letter from Sir William Paget quoted by Rose-Troup. He was a bold man to have written as he did to the Lord Protector; perhaps the fact that he was out of the country on an ambassadorial post is significant. The letter was written on 7 July, when the siege of Exeter had actually started, though Paget clearly did not know this and thought the rebellion could still be snuffed out by determined action.

He may not even have reckoned the West Country revolt worth bothering about, for he speaks specifically of the riots in Buckinghamshire:

> Call together the strongest men in the country and be guided by their authority. Put yourself at the head of the 4000 almayne horsemen [German mercenaries] now idle at Calais, send for your trusty servants, for Lord Ferris and Sir William Herbert to bring horsemen from Wales and such as they dare trust, and for the Earl of Shrewsbury and his followers. With such a force under your command advance into Buckinghamshire, appoint three or four Justices of England to resort to the next town where you rest, join to them local justices and select twenty or thirty of the rankest knaves to come before them. If they come peaceably to justice, let six be hanged of the ripest of them without redemption, the rest to remain in prison. Let the horsemen take enough in the towns to make the rebels smart for their villainy. Take into the King's hands the privileges of offending towns, send some of the chief doers away from their wives to be soldiers at Boulogne or in the North. In such manner make your progress through the country. By this means you shall be dread, which hitherto you are not but of a few that be honest men. By this means you should deliver the King an obedient realm.

Surprisingly, such advice seems not to have been resented, but neither was it acted on. Somerset decided to entrust the army, when he could gather one, to Lord John Russell, a capable, experienced and sometimes brutal soldier who had carved a career, and a fortune, out of services to Henry VIII. He was already Chairman of the Council in the West Parts, almost a viceregal position, and had started to acquire land and property in the area. In the government he held the position of Lord Privy Seal.

By 20 June sums of money were being voted to Russell for the purpose of equipping, transporting and paying a military force; far too small a force for the task, he was certain, but deemed 'adequate' by Somerset and his Treasury officials. The plan was for Russell to go ahead, find himself reasonable quarters and discover what was happening. His troops would follow as soon as all was ready.

He seems to have started out on 25 or 26 June. One would have thought that Somerset, having chosen a senior colleague who was also an experienced general and negotiator, might have trusted him to use his own initiative and judgement, but Russell carried with him a long and rambling instruction which was extraordinarily detailed. Styled a 'Memorial', it was supposed to serve both as a set of instructions to be adhered to and as authorization to call upon the help of various other persons.

According to this astonishing document, Russell was enjoined, amongst many other things, to summon local Justices, to hear their news on the state of the area and to take their advice; when he found anything amiss, to try gentle persuasion at first and only if that failed to use force to bring the people to their senses; if there was a foreign invasion, to repulse it, to improve coastal fortifications and make sure that a watch was kept on coastal areas; to persuade parents that they had to be more responsible about bringing up their children and about the conduct of their servants; to see that the artisan class were kept busy so that they were less likely to indulge in unlawful assembly and riot; to ensure that the king's orders about religion were strictly obeyed. In the event of rumour-mongering or trouble-stirring he was to find out who was responsible and punish them. He was to keep the Privy Council advised at stated intervals about how things were going; to take preachers with him, as army chaplains almost, and they were to persuade the people of the true word, presumably through invitation to friendly pulpits.

As if all this was not enough, a further letter was sent down to Russell three or four days later telling him to appease the multitude at Sampford Courtenay; Somerset was clearly oblivious of the fact that the rebels had long since left Sampford, had fought an action at Crediton and were at that moment preparing their assault on Exeter. Russell was instructed to make Exeter safe. He was to approach the rebels with his cavalry and some 'hagbutes footmen' (soldiers armed with portable guns) and half a dozen or so heavy guns, and while putting on this show of force he was to make a final attempt at conciliation. He was not allowed to construe for himself what this might mean any more than he was allowed, apparently, to make his own plans for the disposition of his troops (which he did not even have). Such futile and infuriating instructions are always ignored, in the event, but they sour relations between a commander in the field and his political masters. Russell's eventual decision to withdraw his support from Somerset when it was most sorely needed may well have had its roots in this sort of instruction, from a man who could not know half of what was happening and did not want to pay for half of what was needed.

But there was more, and Russell must have read on with mounting incredulity and frustration. He was to let the rebels know that their disobedience had been devised by wicked men who meant the king harm; they themselves had been misled by false rumours; if they went home peacefully now, the king would put right their grievances – and no one was more eager and ready to do so than he was – but if they persisted in their rebellion they would be guilty of high treason and punished accordingly.

Russell was further enjoined to show the falseness of the rumours about taxes and payments on sheep and pigs and geese; to reassure the people that they had misunderstood the prayer-book on the subject of baptism, and to exhort them to read the whole book, which would show them the error of their ways; to impress on them that they were being misled by priests who were trying to bring them, and indeed the whole country, into subjection to the pope. If Russell failed to pacify the people he would be at liberty to proceed as he thought best (although Somerset also gave him detailed suggestions as to the use of his troops).

He was then instructed, above all, to capture a certain ringleader who was reported to have taken refuge in the tower of Sampford Courtenay church – it seems that Father Harper is referred to here, although no names are used. This man was to be punished, and he and his associates were to be subjected to terror and the rack to force from them confessions of the names of the ringleaders. Russell was then told to cut off the rebels' food-supplies and reduce them by famine. He was also charged with the execution of two Royal Commissions and a Proclamation. If this left him with time on his hands he was to search out a certain Mr Blaxton of the cathedral body who was suspected of spreading false rumours about the changes in religious worship, to convince him of the errors of his ways and the folly of his past actions and to persuade him to preach to the people in support of the new prayer-book and forms of worship.

Lord Russell was soon given an opportunity to discuss this barrage of instructions with Sir Peter Carew, who was now on his way to London. When Sir Peter dodged the rebel road-block outside Exeter and headed east he had expected to make the two-day journey to London without delay, but on his way up the roads and tracks of Somerset he twice received intelligence that Lord Russell was billeted nearby. At Hinton St George he heard that Russell was at the home of the Paulets, a family that Carew himself knew, and he turned his weary horse aside to check. Within a few minutes the two men had begun to bring each other up to date with events.

Russell explained that he had come ahead of his force and no doubt shared with Carew his fears about the inadequacy of his resources. The two seasoned campaigners will have studied together with dismay, and probably anger, the Lord Protector's letters to Russell (unknown to himself, a few days later Carew would be bringing Russell another, equally ridiculous, package). One thing they will both have agreed on was that Russell was too far from the scene of action where he was and that Mohun's Ottery, the Carews' house near Honiton, would be a more suitable location. Russell was grateful for the offer and determined to move on there as soon as was feasible. Then the commander without an army wrote the first of a series of letters that were to pain and annoy Somerset

45

Lord John Russell

because they asked for more money to be spent. Carew put the letter in his pocket and within an hour had set off again for London.

Sir Peter was a soldier; he was not unfamiliar with the goings-on at court but had little experience of politicians and had not come up the administrators' or courtiers' ladder as Russell had done. He was therefore dumbfounded at his reception when he made his report to the Privy Council. When he related the Crediton incident, the burning of the barns was as much misunderstood by the Privy Councillors as it had been by the peasantry in Devon. There were, it is recorded, exclamations from all sides.

But it was Somerset himself who reacted most angrily to the account of the burning. 'Peaceful and conciliatory measures,' he hissed, 'were to have been used towards these poor deluded people.' He repeated several times that those had been his instructions and that Sir Peter had greatly exceeded them; by burning down the peasants' farms and destroying their livelihoods he had driven them to extremes of action which would now be most difficult and expensive to deal with.

At this point Carew began to realize that he was being made the scapegoat in a situation that had within it the seeds of considerable political unpopularity. He might be only a soldier, but he could see what was happening, and it made him extremely angry. He burst out that he had done only what the king's warrant specifically authorized him to do. When one or two of the Council begged leave to doubt that fact, he produced the battered document from his pocket and pointed to the final passage: '.. if any manner person after this our writing, pardon, and commandment shall eftsoons attempt to repugne or resist our Godly proceedings in the laws by us and our parliament made by gathering or assembling in companies or otherwise to apprehend the same and to see our laws and statutes duly and severely executed against all such offenders as appertaineth'.

Carew's feeling of triumph was apparent. Somerset looked trapped. Perhaps he had exceeded his brief, or his powers, in providing this warrant for Sir Peter, especially as it sat ill with his consistent demands for a conciliatory approach. But the Council closed ranks, sensing damage to their collective credibility. Rich, the Lord Chancellor, made a shabby attempt to argue things out. He demanded to examine the document, then declared that it was only a letter and that for action as extreme as Sir Peter had taken he would have needed the king's commission under the broad seal, a much more specific authorization. He tried threats, too, and suggested that Sir Peter ought to be hanged for what he had done. The latter continued to protest and pointed out the wording at the end of the document and the royal seal. The Lord Chancellor bluffed a little longer and explained with feigned weariness that Carew should have had the authority of the whole Council.

'And I have,' retorted the knight; he forced them to face the precise words: '.. by the advice of our entirely beloved uncle, the Lord Protector, and the rest of the privy council'. Then Sir Peter hit upon a telling phrase: 'If my Lord the King and the Duke's Grace say they have that authority it is enough for me, unless you tell me that my Lord Protector has no power in this matter.'

The Councillors were unsure how to proceed. Many of them wished to attack Somerset for his inconsistency and for his arbitrary action, which had left them looking and feeling foolish, but they did not intend to have this row in public. They therefore adjourned the meeting and Sir Peter withdrew. When they met later they decided, though fierce things were said by the faction Warwick led, that the matter must drop and that Carew was too valuable a man, with too much local knowledge, not to be used in putting the troubles to rights. They read the letter from Russell Carew had brought them and wrote a reply promising speedy help. Carew was once more asked to ride west, taking with him the Council's reply.

But one brush with politicians, even if he had got the best of it, had made Carew wary. While he was in a position of relative strength he wanted to make quite sure that he could clear himself of any charge of treachery or excess zeal if it later became convenient to have somebody to blame. Before he would even think of putting spurs to his horse, he wanted letters from the king in Council stating that he had not acted *ultra vires*. This he demanded and received, and he set off again, a little like a glorified messenger-boy, perhaps, but with the satisfaction of knowing he had stood up to the highest in the land, the most cunning in the land, and bested them.

Meanwhile it is important to the overall picture to consider the religious attitude of the people of Exeter. The city was close to being surrounded and in a few days would be under siege. The citizens' morale and the degree of their determination to resist must, one feels, have been linked to what they thought about the religious changes that were the cause of the unrest outside the walls.

Rose-Troup describes Exeter as being 'then, as long afterwards, the Metropolis of the West'. It is easy to forget, now, just how true this was. The reduction and capture of Plymouth in the Western Rebellion was not very important, yet if Exeter had fallen, the whole of the West Country, and very likely the whole nation, would have been in turmoil. Plymouth had significance as a seaport, but to a limited degree. Henry VIII had quite recently founded the Royal Navy and Plymouth was only just starting her climb towards the importance she later reached. The intellectual, ecclesiastical, financial and commercial capital of the West was Exeter. Within the city the cathedral close held the key to the first two of those claims of pre-eminence, and it was also the centre of suspicion as far as those promoting the New Learning were concerned. It could hardly have been otherwise, given the conservative nature of the people, and the general age of the clergy.

One interesting question which has yet to be satisfactorily answered lies in the following paradox: the chief citizens of Exeter, a high proportion of the common people and the vast majority of the clergy openly or covertly favoured the cause of the rebels outside the walls, yet all three groups gave general support and in many cases active help in the defence of the city against their co-religionists outside the gates. Why should this have been so?

Part of the answer must lie in the real horror of ordinary people at that time for the crime of treason. Irrespective of the rights and wrongs of individual cases, to take up arms against the Lord's Anointed was almost universally viewed with repugnance. Part of the answer will certainly lie in the mayor's decision to back the king in spite of his own preferences, and in the mayor's popularity and skilful leadership.

The consciences of the cathedral clerics were another matter. The benefices they enjoyed made life pleasant and undemanding. They tended to let events wash over them and ride with the sway of events. The Vicar of Bray's pragmatic attitude was widespread long before that gentleman gave his name to it, and seems to have been prevalent from the top down.

John Veysey, who became Bishop of Exeter in 1519, had learned caution and diplomacy in his close liaison with Henry VIII's court. An intimate of Wolsey – in whose set he had been in their Magdalen days – he was prominent when Wolsey received his cardinal's hat, yet sailed on serenely when the great man was disgraced. He carried out numerous tasks connected with the consolidation of the new faith, but was tutor for some time to the Princess Mary. And although he assisted at the consecration of the first Protestant archbishop, he was eventually recalled by Mary Tudor to take on the see of Exeter again in the interests of the old faith. The truth must be that he was clever enough and unscrupulous enough to be valuable to the right people at the right time, and many at Exeter followed his example.

One reason why the cathedral canons had so little regard for the reformed religion, even if they had to pay lip-service to it, was the extreme unpopularity of the dean that the royal command had imposed on them a dozen years before. Simon Heynes, once Vice-Chancellor of Cambridge University, was installed as a canon on 4 June 1537, and when the resistance of the other canons was finally overcome by the king's insistence, he was elected dean on 16 July. Even Henry VIII could hardly move with more indelicate haste than that.

The canons knew, of course, that Heynes was the king's man, put there to see that things went as the king thought they should, but they could not have expected that he would make himself as objectionable as he did. From the start he flouted their customs, refused to make the contributions traditionally demanded of the dean, and showed himself personally rapacious and high-handed to a degree. The squabbles between Heynes and the other canons were still going on after the 1549 revolt was over and done with.

Nor is there evidence to suggest that the common people were welcoming the new religious laws. The behaviour of the mob when poor Thomas Dusgate was burned at Livery Dole for fixing anti-papal notices to the cathedral door certainly does not suggest it, nor does the vigorous reaction of the five ladies of Exeter who took the law into their own hands in the Church of St Nicholas's Priory.

The Royal Commissioners were intent on suppressing the Priory and, being unable to recruit local workmen to do the sacrilegious work of breaking up the rood-loft there, they had employed two Breton travelling workmen to do it. These two had prudently locked the door while they were at work, but this was not enough to stop the ladies, whose names are given in Oliver's *Bishops of Exeter* as Joan Reeve, Elizabeth Gladfield, Agnes Colleton, Alice Miller and Joan Reed. Furious at the reports they had heard, the women burst down the door and went for the workmen. An alderman tried to intervene to keep the peace but they gave him a buffet which put him out of action and then gave chase to the Bretons. One of them was so frightened that he leapt from the window, breaking several ribs. Such stalwart ladies will not easily have been persuaded to the new faith, yet they stood resolutely to the defence of their city in the trial that was so soon to be upon them.

$$—7—$$

Exeter:
The Siege Begins

Word came to the rebels as they toiled from Crediton towards Exeter that Mayor John Blackaller had rejected their second demand for the surrender of the city. The news was surprising as the mayor and many of the civic dignitaries were known personally to support the old faith, but the words Blackaller had used left no room for doubt that he intended to put his duty to the king and to his city above his own religious leanings. Hoker quotes these words from his reply: '... they in their doings were wicked and bad men, and they did and would refute them enemies and rebels against God, their King and country, and so renounced them ...'.

Even so, Arundell and his followers did not really think they would have to mount a protracted siege. Even if the mayor and his councillors felt that they must at least make a show of loyalty to the king, there were known to be many living within the city, especially in the Southgate area, and outside the walls in Southernhay, who held to the old rites and would not want to stand out against their co-religionists. Some of them would also remember Perkin Warbeck's siege in 1497 or have heard tell of the great hardships and damage of those earlier days. Morale in Exeter would not be high and there were persistent reports that no extra stocks of food had been taken in to withstand a prolonged attack.

In those last days of June rumours spread wildly amongst the rebel force. The king was dead. There was to be a poll-tax on sheep. All food was to be taxed in an effort to crush the uprising. Russell and his troops were skulking near Honiton, afraid to meet the insurgents in battle. Those who supported the old faith had taken over Exeter and the gates would be opened. Hundreds who supported the rebels had left the city and were on their way to join them.

In fact, the last was substantially true; there had been considerable defections in the forty-eight hours before the siege began, though this probably worked against the rebels' interests in the long run. Their supporters might well have proved more effective inside the walls, and the chances of an uprising forcing a surrender would certainly have been enhanced if they had stayed inside. The food-supply would also have run out sooner had there been more mouths to feed.

On Tuesday 2 July 1549 the resolute Mayor Blackaller ordered the five great gates of the city to be barred. At first light there had been sightings of the advancing forces and he and his fellow councillors had donned their robes and insignia and hurried out on to the wall near the West Gate. Across the river, beyond the church of St Thomas, they saw the glint of sunlight on armour and on the gold and silver of religious objects.

In his heart the mayor must have been much less sure of the outcome than one would have guessed from the brave show he put on. The council itself was quite seriously divided, and the decision to uphold the mayoral view would probably be maintained only as long as things went reasonably well. It was impossible to tell who amongst the citizens would remain loyal to the new king, as opposed to the old faith, and many of them were uncertain how members of their own households would react. There was the added worry and lingering doubt that in one sense the rebels were right. Henry VIII had agreed that the new measures need not be enforced until his son reached the age of royal competence, and many Church leaders, notably the Bishop of Winchester, were urging the wisdom of waiting. But the Lord Protector had become impatient and was determined to force matters through.

Because the rebels knew that their best chance of having the city tamely surrendered to them lay in playing upon the religious anxieties of the defenders, the approaching army had at its head a procession that, employing every device of pomp and ceremony, was designed to tug at the heart-strings and touch the consciences of those who watched from the walls. At the very front, fluttering in the July breeze, was the banner of the 'five wounds', prominent in all the rebellions against the reformed religion. Then came rows of priests chanting solemnly in full regalia, and amongst them, under a gorgeously embroidered canopy, was the sacred pyx, round which acolytes swung censers. Clouds of the old familiar incense rose to reproach the nostrils of those on the battlements above, just as their ears were assailed by the chanting of the choirboys wearing cottas and cassocks and carrying the huge processional candles.

When they were close to the red sandstone walls there was a flourish of trumpets to call attention to a herald who stepped forward and called on

Banner showing the badge of the five wounds, a symbol of faith for both the Pilgrimage of Grace and the Western Rebellion

the city to join them against the new and unlawful order. He added the threat that if they did not, the rebels would enter the city and despoil it. But the moment of hesitation and doubt seemed to be past, and John Blackaller himself shouted back a defiant answer before hurrying along to the Guildhall to finalize plans for Exeter's defence.

Many of the ordinary citizens, however, stayed on the ramparts to see what the enemy would do, and fairly ripe were the insults and promises that flew backward and forward even if, for the moment, it was only verbal warfare. The rebels were the more vociferous. They would starve the citizens out of Exeter like rats from a sewer, they promised. They guaranteed to be in the city by such and such a date, and would need horses and carts to transport all the loot they would take. There were threats of rape, too, amongst those of pillage, and some almost good-natured banter, until arrows whistled and thumped too close for comfort. The besiegers moved back out of range while the townsfolk dispersed to consider gloomily the hardships to be expected in a siege.

By next morning it was clear that the attackers had spread out in a circle (as Cotton and Woolacombe have gleaned from the municipal records): '... from St David's Down to St Sidwell's church, across the wide wastes of the Southern-Hay, even to the Southgate along the open banks and flats by the river from the Watergate past Westgate to Snayle tower'.

But initially, at least, they were thinly spread. The historian Hoker, who was an eye-witness, reckoned that there were but two thousand of the enemy on 2 July, but that more arrived almost every day once the siege had started in earnest. There were estimated to be as many as ten thousand of them, at their most numerous, and even if this is an exaggeration one must remember that the total population of Exeter at that time was little more than three thousand.

Meanwhile the mayor and his brethren were wasting no time in planning the defence and getting everything ready. Every piece of armour in the city was called in and collected for the common use. Men were mustered, the few real soldiers in the town were given the job of drilling and instructing male citizens, captains were appointed to every ward and each section of the wall was allotted wardens by day and watchmen by night. Cannon were placed at tactical points on the ramparts and vast, wide-mouthed port pieces (highly inaccurate but devastating at short range when charged with all conceivable missiles by the bucket-load) were in position to guard their respective gates. At the foot of St Edmund's Bridge they erected a *chevaux de frise*, a barrier with scores of murderously sharp spikes. Most important of all, they managed, while in the process of putting the city on a war footing, to strengthen morale and inspire a sense of purpose and comradeship within the walls, and these they were certain to need before long.

One cause of great anxiety to the defenders, and of encouragement to the besiegers, was the apparently inexplicable delaying of Russell and the royal force at Honiton. We know now that Russell felt he needed a stronger army before he moved, and that the government was determined that the whole operation should be carried out at minimum expense, but around Exeter they knew only that he was not moving. There have been suggestions that he was wasting time on secret instructions from London, but this seems highly unlikely; the correspondence clearly indicates that he was not prepared to move until the Protector provided adequate resources. This correspondence was not available to the rebels, of course, and the delay was widely interpreted as being due to fear, and wilder and wilder rumours followed each other as the resolve of the rebels hardened.

Early in the siege, in fact, the defenders were in mortal peril, but it was some days before they realized it. Lacking the equipment and training for more general means of assault, the attackers fell back on a method in which the Cornish tin miners in particular were both experienced and skilful. They began to tunnel under the wall near the West Gate that looks down on the Exe Bridge and the river. They carefully kept their men away from the area so as not to draw attention to what they were up to. When rumours and reports of subterranean noises began to alarm the citizens, John Newcombe, on a visit to Exeter from Teignmouth and himself a tinner, volunteered to take counteraction.

From the walls the people watched in fascination as Newcombe carried out a wide shallow pan of water. For half a morning he moved it here and there, tracing the line and extent of the mining by the tremors on the water's surface. When he had the information he needed he went back into the city and told the townspeople that there was no time to lose. With a team of volunteers he constructed a countermine from inside with feverish haste. So accurate was he that when he finally broke through a tiny hole he could see the Cornishmen loading gunpowder and pitch into a chamber at the end of their shaft. The great explosion they were preparing would undoubtedly have brought down a large section of the wall between the West Gate and the Water Gate, not far from the road that now runs down to the Customs House and the quay. According to contemporary reports Newcombe even overheard the date and time arranged for the explosion.

It is highly likely that if Newcombe had not happened to be in Exeter and to be detained there by the siege, the city would have been successfully stormed and the course of West Country history would have been changed. As it was, he quickly outlined his plan and the authorities hastened to carry out his instructions. A drainage channel was built into Newcombe's mine and all the streams and drains on the hillside above were made to run that way and lightly dammed. Then every householder who lived on that hill was instructed to provide a hogshead of water and stand it by his front door. At a given signal every tub was overturned to fill the gutters; the dams were swept aside and a great and growing torrent of water rushed down the hill and drowned the enemy mine. There are lurid accounts of a thunderstorm of particular violence that broke at the same instant, but it is as well to be suspicious of such awe-inspiring coincidences; sixteenth-century historians were always very partial to their own view of events and the idea that the Almighty was active on their side made people feel their actions were justified.

The attackers then gave up the mining attempt. Since they lacked heavy siege-pieces with which the walls might have been breached, and were unsure of their men's training and ability with scaling-ladders, the rebels were left with only two options: fire, or starving the city into sub-mission. Rejecting the latter as too lengthy a business, they set out to burn down the wooden gates of the city, by a method that had almost succeeded in the Perkin Warbeck siege of fifty years before. This involved piling a cart high with old hay and pushing it in front of you up to the gates, where you would quickly set it on fire. In theory, if you did it right, the bulk of the hay and the cart protected you on the approach run, and the sudden surge of flame as the hay caught fire made it hard for the marksmen to pick you off as you ran back.

At the West Gate and the South Gate, however, the would-be arsonists were spotted and some of them were killed. Hoker describes it vividly: '. . . the great porte peces were chardged wth greate bages of flynte stones and hayle shote and as they were aprochinge vnto the gate the gate would be secretlie opened and the saide porte peces dyshardged and so they were spoyled dyverse of theime'.

Jenkins, writing his *History of Exeter* in 1806, remembers seeing one of these 'porte peces' at the East Gate – near what is now the South West Gas Show-room: 'One of those port pieces (in the author's memory) was remaining and laid on the left side of the passage under the East Gate: it was composed of flat iron bars, strongly hooped together with iron (similar to a cask) and was near twelve feet in length, and twelve inches diameter at the mouth . . . it did not ever seem to have been fixed on a carriage as it had no trunnions'.

But it was another defensive ploy that robbed the burning of the gates of usefulness. Instead of trying to put out the flames, the townspeople threw down more dry fuel and made even fiercer fires which themselves formed effective barriers. When, on some occasions, the attackers did force their way through charred and smouldering woodwork they found that the defenders had thrown up earthworks inside the gates and were able to bring enfilade fire to bear with great effect on those who ventured through them. Hayward, in his biography of Edward VI, describes it thus: '. . . for the defenders added fuel to the flames, preventing the near approach of the enemy until they had cast up a strong rampire, shaped like a half moon, so

56

that when the seditious pushed their way in they were slain from the corners like dogs'.

Later the townspeople kept some of the gates open, relying instead on huge bonfires they kept burning in the gateways, and on the defences within, for their protection.

Although the holders of the city were able to match the enemy's tactics and to foil their various plans, as the weeks went by they became increasingly at risk from the dissensions within. An example of this was the great row over nocturnal sallies into enemy lines. The mayor and some of the military commanders had become anxious over the scope and frequency of these expeditions, which seemed to be taking place at the whim of local commanders eager to win glory and riches.

The most active of the local commanders was an overweening ruffian called Bernard Duffield in the service of Lord Russell, and ever keen to take advantage of the fact that he worked for a man people were afraid of. He was in charge of Russell's establishment, Bedford House, which was like a little castle and stood near the wall just south of the East Gate. It had a postern in the main wall which was a useful exit at night and offered a better line of retreat, in terms of cover, than most of the other sally-ports. On one of these expeditions Duffield and his men had killed several of the enemy, and captured guns, weapons and goods. But they also suffered casualties. John Symonds, a cook, died of his wounds, we are told; and John Drake, who had been the city's official receiver the year before, was shot through both cheeks with an arrow 'which he brought back into the city with him'.

Excited by his success, Duffield planned a series of such escapades but was taken to task by John Courtenay, younger son of Sir William of Powderham, and already a soldier of experience. He argued that sorties should be made in furtherance of a general defence policy and not entered into lightly or for amusement or profit. Duffield was furious and appealed to the mayor, but that worthy supported Courtenay and ruled that henceforth sallies could be undertaken only in emergencies and at the specific instructions of the general or 'chief captain'.

Duffield, never in very firm control of his temper, became almost apoplectic at this ruling, which he considered a slur on his honour and on his competence. He began to shout and swear at the mayor, or as Hoker put it: '... by continuing of talks fell out in loud and disordered speeches'. John Blackaller had to act to maintain his authority and Duffield was put in the city gaol to cool off.

However, Duffield's daughter, a fierce young lady who had clearly inherited the family temperament, came up to the mayor without ceremony and demanded most imperiously that her father be released at once. When this was denied her, Frances Duffield immediately: '... waxed so warm that not only she used very unseemly terms and speeches unto the Mayor but also, contrary to the modesty and shamefacedness required in a woman, especially young and unmarried, ran most violently upon him, and strake him in the face'.

Hoker's account is graphic enough, and certainly those looking on were outraged at what they had witnessed. One or two of them over-reacted somewhat hysterically and rushed out shouting that the mayor had been killed. Someone ordered the ringing of the great Common Bell, which was sounded only for extreme emergencies, and everyone ran to assemble at the Guildhall, buckling on their armour as they went.

Meanwhile the stormy Frances had fled in the confusion and was again inside Bedford House. John Blackaller had the sense to swallow his pride. A full-scale riot at this juncture could have been a disaster. He made light of his injuries, but had to call on all his powers of persuasion to stop the enraged mob from going into Bedford House and dragging Frances out. Exeter was lucky in its mayor at this time of crisis. He may not have been a soldier but he showed good military judgement. He also had presence and authority, and the good sense to see that he must use both to prevent disturbances that could so easily have been fatal in a situation where loyalties were cruelly divided.

—8—

Besieging the City

Outside the city, while they did not have the hardships of hunger to worry about, the rebel commanders had several causes for concern. Besieging a city is exciting as long as active assault measures are in process. While you are mining, burning gates, breaching walls or attacking with scaling-ladders there is a sense of purpose and a focus of interest; but when you have tried all or some of these, and have settled down to the long wait that may bring conflict within the walls, or surrender from hunger or thirst, things go differently.

Exeter's defenders, constantly in danger, ever alert to what the rebels might try next, kept their sense of unity and their morale because of that danger. Outside the city walls even trained troops found it difficult to maintain discipline and motivation when there was little to do and each day too closely resembled the day before.

Hayward's account speaks of assaults on the walls being beaten back, and Arundell's men certainly made some scaling-ladders, but there is no evidence in Hoker that they used them very often. Their efforts to burn the gates were not productive, though they were, technically, successful. The most promising line of attack had been the mining and that had almost succeeded. It is hard to understand, looking back, why they did not mine again, possibly in two places at once; if they had concentrated on an area of wall where there was no natural hill on the other side – such as round the East Gate – they would at least have known that John Newcombe's scheme to drown their mine could not be repeated. Perhaps the prospect of the sheer physical work involved was unpopular, perhaps the miners themselves were drowned in the first attempt and feared a repeat, perhaps the expenditure in powder was prohibitive; whatever the reason, the method best suited to the skill and experience of the attackers was abandoned.

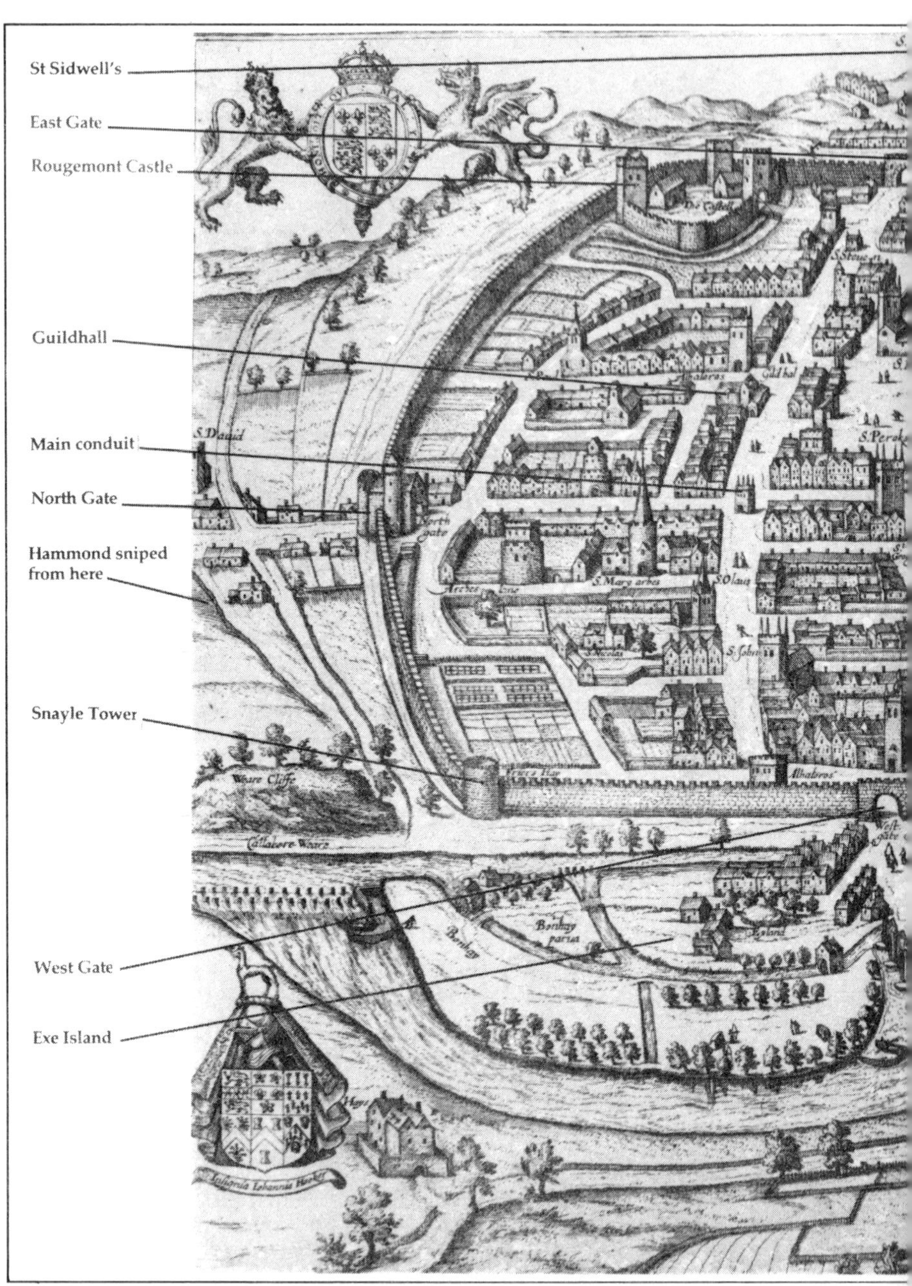

Hoker's map of Exeter

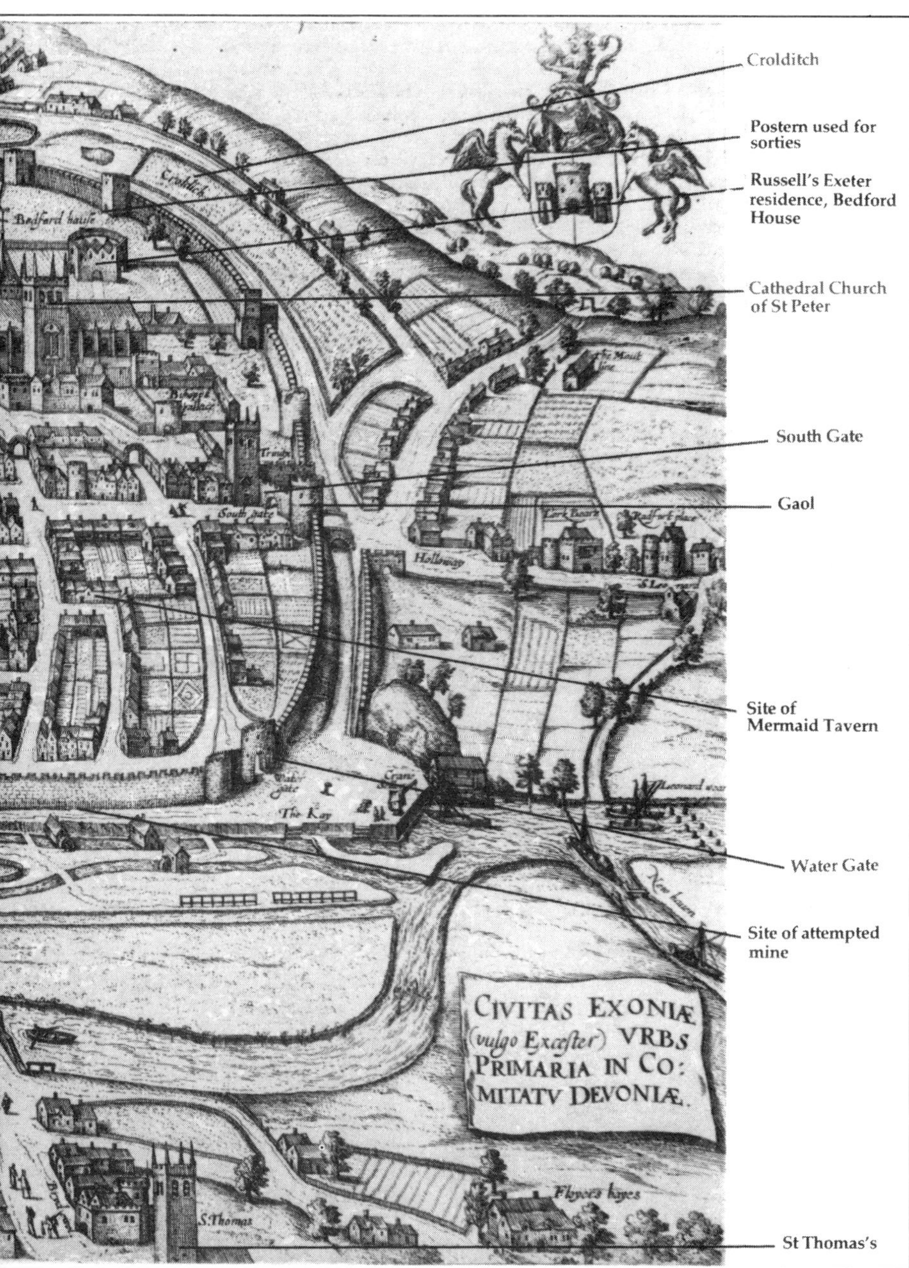

Crolditch
Postern used for sorties
Russell's Exeter residence, Bedford House
Cathedral Church of St Peter
South Gate
Gaol
Site of Mermaid Tavern
Water Gate
Site of attempted mine
St Thomas's
Bedford house
Crolditch
South Gate
The Kay
CIVITAS EXONIÆ (vulgo Excester) VRBS PRIMARIA IN CO: MITATV DEVONIÆ.
S.Thomas

No doubt the two long-term levers of insurrection and famine seemed likely to succeed. The rebels knew that the majority of those within the city were sympathetic to their religious beliefs. Surely they would soon rise and open the gates in welcome, especially as life became increasingly harassing and hard as the siege continued. And if this did not happen, well, the city was known not to be provisioned for a siege, since they had not had sufficient warning and none of the people round about had supplied extra food during the last day or two before the gates closed. Time seemed on the rebels' side, for there was still no sign of the king's army. Its commander was skulking somewhere over in East Devon and he had no worthwhile force, anyway. The government had too much else on its plate and had obviously abandoned Exeter to its fate.

Thus they comforted themselves as they manned their barricades and watched by night to make sure no food was smuggled in to relieve the city. Once or twice the defenders had captured cattle on their sorties, but Arundell was determined at all costs to prevent any repetition of this. He had hoped that a shortage of water would have aided his cause, but it seems that there were, and indeed still are numerous springs of sweet water in different parts of the city and this was never a problem for the defenders.

In the tower of St Sidwell's Church were imprisoned for the duration of the siege local gentry who, having been stopped at the road-blocks or found on their property, had refused to join or support the rebels. The records imply that Mr Walter Raleigh, who was amongst the prisoners, was singled out for less sympathetic treatment than the others. Perhaps his previous rescue by the seafarers or his rather officious interference with the old woman at Clyst St Mary had now told against him. The church was very close to the East Gate and the prisoners must have had a grandstand view of the progress of the siege if they were allowed the run of the tower.

The leaders of the attackers certainly seemed to understand a good deal of the psychology of siege warfare and they induced their followers to make life as nasty and as uncomfortable for the townspeople as they could. One method was noise, and by staging great false alarms during the night, with no actual intention to attack but with all the trappings of a full-scale assault, they robbed the inhabitants of sleep and wreaked havoc on their nerves.

Also there was sniping. Although the walls of Exeter were high enough, and kept in good repair at this period, sniping was possible in certain areas. The city is built on a little hill and some buildings, such as The Mermaid tavern, not far inside the walls near the Water Gate, were vulnerable, as could clearly be seen from outside the walls. The Mermaid stood where there is now a housing development called Mermaid Court, near Preston

Street. It had a fine assembly room upstairs and was a popular place to stay, favoured especially by merchants. You could sit on the balcony drinking your ale, and look down on your ship bobbing at its moorings at the quay beyond the city wall. If the residents could look down, of course, it is certain that the enemy could look up. The balcony of The Mermaid was not much in use during these grim weeks.

In other places there is high ground outside the walls, on the Pinhoe and Pennsylvania sides and near St David's Church, for example, areas then outside the city limits. The besiegers had no heavy artillery with which they might have breached the walls, but they had several lighter pieces and made good use of them. There were places where the defenders erected barricades or mounds of stone to obstruct the sight-lines of the snipers, who in their turn spent their powder and energy destroying them so that they could carry on annoying the citizens.

For one man called Smith it was rather more than an annoyance. He was standing at the door of his house in Northgate Street enjoying the July sunshine and may have idly noticed a flash up on St David's Down. He cannot have heard the crash of the gun, however, because the ball reached him first and left him bleeding to death in the gutter.

Hoker is graphic in his description of the difficulties of life under the sniping:

> ... the rebels would keep themselves close in sundry houses in the suburbs near the walls and would so watch the garrets that if any within the city would look out at the garrets they with their shot did shrewdly gall and annoy as also killed divers of the city watching and warding within upon the walls which was the cause that some part of the said suburbs was burned and some part beaten down and spoiled, and so drave the rebels out of those holes: besides this they had in sundry places their great ordnances so set and placed that in certain streets and places none could go but in peril and danger of their shot, in which their devices were choked by making of certain mounts to shadow the streets from the same ....

Some reports indicate that the specially skilful gunner up on the Down by St David's Church was none other than John Hammond, the blacksmith from Woodbury who had been in charge of the gun on the bridge at Clyst St Mary and who had been prevented by Hugh Osborne from blowing Sir Peter Carew to pieces a few weeks earlier.

By an irony of fate, Hammond – if it were he – had another chance to alter history, but his hand was stayed again. He had killed a number of

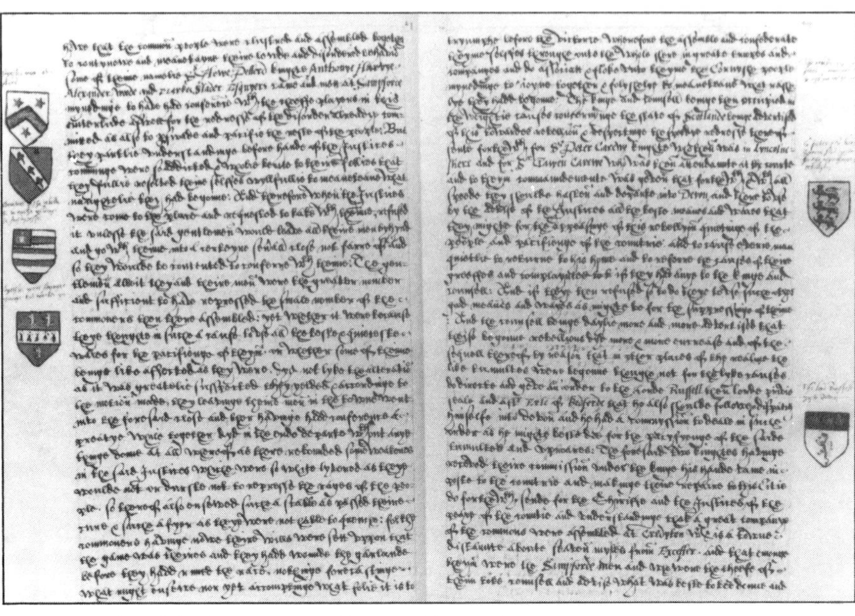

Pages from the original manuscript of Hoker's history of Exeter

people besides poor Mr Smith and he was tremendously excited by a plan he had thought up to reduce the city by fire. Although in aiming at specific targets he was limited to streets that ran more or less towards the North Gate, Queen Street, Mary Arches Street, etc., he could reach most parts of the city if aim were not critical. He boasted to friends that, using red-hot shot, he could have the whole city on fire in the space of four hours, and as nearly all the houses were then timber-framed this may have been no idle boast. His friends certainly took it seriously, and a date was fixed to carry out the plan.

On the appointed day, there was a brisk wind blowing to fan the flames, and hundreds of interested spectators began to gather up on St David's Down an hour or two before the time announced for the event. There seems to have been an air of fiesta and gaiety not entirely appropriate to the gravity of the occasion. Then suddenly there burst upon the scene the sturdy little figure of the Vicar of St Thomas, Father Welsh, together with a band of his parishioners. He was in a determined and angry mood and seemed outraged at the plan that had been made.

This short, thickset Cornishman was very popular in the area, partly because of his athletic skills, no doubt. Though small he was famous as a wrestler and was a good shot with a longbow, crossbow and gun. He was a

64

tough little character and a good sport, but a serious man too. He was a strong supporter of the old faith.

On this occasion the vicar had come to spoil the people's sport and some of them resented it. Only a man of his popularity and strength of character, and one who was known to them as a true supporter of their cause, could have got away with it. Hoker records that Welsh made a spirited speech, and quotes him; one can imagine him standing in front of the gun, defying the gun-layer: '... I will in no wise suffer so lewd an act and wicked a thing to be done. Do what you can by policy, by force, or by dint of sword, and I will join you and do my uttermost, but to burn the city, which would be hurtful to all and profitable to none, I will not consent thereto, but will withstand you with all my power'. Hoker continues, with growing respect: '... so stout was he in this matter that he stopped them of their further enterprising of so wicked a fact'. And although the gun-layer Hammond continued to ply his trade as a sniper, there was no more talk of heated shot or incendiarism.

With so many champions of and sympathizers with the old ways inside the city there was bound to be much devious intrigue and secret communication, and indeed there were regular lines of information both between Lord Russell and the city's mayor and between Catholic supporters inside the walls and rebels outside. Both messages and bribes were conveyed, the rebels attaching messages to arrows and firing them over the walls in the direction of known sympathizers and into areas where they knew their friends lived.

A number of plots were hatched in this way, perhaps the most celebrated being the bribing of some soldiers billeted in Rougemont Castle to open the North Gate, of which they were to be in charge on the night in question. The arrangement was that the guards would open the gate, under pretence of checking it, for a few moments every hour during the first part of the night; a number of rebels would slip in each time this happened until there were about fifty of them inside. They would pretend to overpower the guard and open the gate. But the townspeople's leaders got to hear of the plot and had a substantial force standing by. When the fifty or so rebels were in, they and the treacherous soldiers were all overpowered and marched off to prison.

Hayward speaks of furious attacks on the gates and walls, more and more desperate as time began to run out, but there is no evidence to suggest that they actually broke in at any point, as did happen in the Perkin Warbeck siege. On that occasion the besiegers broke in two or possibly three times and there was fighting in the streets. They burned the North Gate and forced an entry, but discovered that Northgate Street constituted a strong defensive position because the attackers had to fight uphill with defenders on both sides above them pouring down fire and missiles.

The most nearly successful attack by Warbeck's men, though, was through the East Gate, which they broke down or blew in, and, weathering the first blasts from the wide-mouthed port pieces filled with sharp flints and scrap metal, they forced their way down what is now the High Street as far as the corner of Castle Street. With several hundred of them pouring through the gate, it looked at one moment as if the Cornishmen might win the day and take the city. We are told that the Earl of Devon, Lord Courtenay, was staying that morning at the house of the Blackfriars, where Bedford Circus now is, and on hearing the affray ran with his servants to help beat back the insurgents.

In fact there was also a Courtenay staying in Exeter during the 1549 rising, and apparently he too gave good service. Cotton and Woolcombe tell us: '... of the county gentlemen four only had the patriotism to remain at the post of danger, and they rendered signal service by their military knowledge and habits of command. There names were Blewett, Beauchampe, Fortescue and Courtenay of Powderham'.

The comment is somewhat unfair. Had they forgotten that the day before the siege started the mayor had asked all gentry with estates near by to leave the city because there would not be enough food for all their supporters and followers? When the gates thundered shut it was largely a matter of chance who was inside and who tried to dodge the road-blocks and get home as the mayor had requested.

Among the many attempts at espionage there was one in which a man was caught red-handed. The way the rebels dealt with him was later used by the king's men to justify far worse brutalities of their own. The man's name was Kingwell; originally a tinner from Chagford, he was in the service of a Tavistock Justice of the Peace called John Charles. Kingwell was caught slipping out of one of the postern gates at night with letters from his master to Lord Russell.

He might have escaped serious harm after his capture if he had been a little more prudent. He could have argued, after all, that he was carrying a message on the instructions of the man that employed him. But this he did not do and from the contemporary account it is obvious that he was a zealot and insisted on talking himself into trouble:

> ... he was earnest in the reformed religion which was then termed the King's proceedings and an enemy of the Popish state ... they used all the devices they could to recover him to their opinions, sometimes fair words sometimes with threatenings and sometimes with imprisonment:

but still he inveighed against them calling them rebels and traitors both against God and the King and 'foreprofeceide' unto them that destruction and confusion would be the end and the reward of their doings.

It does seem that every effort was made to give Kingwell the chance to repent but he went out of his way to revile his captors. Some sort of hearing occurred, though there appears to be no evidence for Rose-Troup's assertion that a formal trial was held. At this point Parson Welsh must have lost patience with the man, who had probably been captured in the parish of St Thomas and was therefore under his jurisdiction in a way, for, still shouting his defiance, Kingwell was taken to a great elm tree that stood on Exe Island, and hanged.

With typical partiality, Hoker tries to equate the killing of this one man, who, caught in the very act of what was seen as espionage, chose a noisy martyr's death even though he was given every chance of saving himself, with the later killing in cold blood by the Protestant side of hundreds of prisoners, for reasons of little more than convenience. Hoker also gives this execution as justification for the barbarities later unleashed on the Revd Welsh.

Exe Island, where the hanging took place, lies outside the West Gate and was formed by branches of the river and by leats and channels constructed for fish-traps and to drive mills of various kinds. The island had been in the hands of the Courtenay family, who enjoyed privileges that had intensely annoyed successive mayors and city councils, because the place was exempt from their taxes and outside their control. After the family disgrace of 1538, when the Marquis of Exeter was executed for treason, the island came into the possession of the Crown. The civic authorities of Exeter made several attemps to buy it from the king, but without success. (The fact that they have it now is due to the siege which forms so important a part of our story.)

At about the time of Kingwell's hanging the rebels sent the Lord Protector a final version of their demands – the terms, in fact, on which they would be prepared to call the whole thing off and go home in peace. They had made a much shorter list at the Sampford Courtenay flare-up, but the terms they now presented were more comprehensive, and not entirely of a religious nature. It is hard to imagine how they could have believed the government would seriously consider granting their demands, unless it was in imminent danger of being overthrown.

As before, there were stipulations about the faith of their forefathers being restored; the standard demand for the restoration of the Six Articles, by which Henry VIII had sought to restrict religious changes after his death; the mass in Latin, and the celebration without interruption; the reservation of the host; the celebration of the mass in the old form; baptism on any day, and holy bread and water. All these were much as before, but there now began to creep in extra demands which suggest that the rebels really thought they were on the very edge of military triumph and in a strong bargaining position. For example, they added to their demand for the reservation of the host the following belligerent words: '... and they whiche will not thereto consent, we wyl have them dye lyke heretykes against the holy Catholic fayth'. They also stipulated the return of images to the churches, something that had not been mentioned before.

The rebels repeated the old complaint about the new service being like a Christmas game, and the regular grievance of the Cornish: 'Whereof certen of vs vnderstade no Englysh'. They demanded new things too: prayers at every service for the souls in purgatory, the withdrawal from service of the new Bible in English (the Coverdale and Tyndale version, presumably), and the release of Dr Moreman and Dr Crispin and the return of their livings; they also wanted Cardinal Pole to be pardoned and sent to Rome as the king's representative at the Vatican. Their three final demands were political in a different sense. The first was for a law that no gentleman could have more than one servant to wait on him unless he was prepared to pay heavily for the privilege. The next was for a partial restoration of the plundered religious houses; the rebels stipulated that half the proceeds of the dissolutions should be recovered from those who now enjoyed them and that this be augmented by half the offerings collected in church alms boxes for the next seven years, the money raised thus to be used to establish – on the site of the former chief abbeys of the region – two institutions in each county where devout persons could be supported to pray for the king and the commonwealth! (One cannot help wondering who was to have the privilege of administering this impossible and unpopular task and just how the ill-gotten gains, now often long since spent, were to be prized from the outraged owners). The final requirement was for a safe conduct for Humphrey Arundell and for Henry Bray, Mayor of Bodmin, though why only these two leaders were selected is not clear.

Such were the terms. From them one can deduce that although the priests were no doubt the chief drafters and prompters of demands, lay grievances were beginning to make themselves felt and considerations of social justice were starting to press for attention. It has been pointed out that the tone in which these demands were couched verges on the insolent, which indicates that at the time they were drawn up Exeter's besiegers really did expect the city to fall to them at any moment.

—**9**—

The Long Wait,
and Carnage at Blood Meadow

If, judging from the tone of their demands to the king, it appears that the besiegers' morale was high, we know that within the beleaguered city morale was harder to maintain. To enquire into the spirits of the king's army, the third element in this tableau, is not easy, since it did not at this stage really exist. Its commander, Lord Russell, had been appointed, however, and he was not very far from despair.

Russell had come to the Carews' house as suggested, but nothing else had yet gone according to plan. He was beginning to think that Honiton was a little closer to the centre of disaffection than he really cared to be, especially with no proper force at his command. And he was frustrated; not just because he was making little progress, but because he seemed actually to be going backwards.

According to instructions he had, as soon as he arrived, organized meetings and levées of the local gentry who were known to remain loyal to the king. He had explained his situation: he was short of money but had been promised more; horsemen and foot-soldiers would be sent by the government very soon, and artillery and supplies would not be long delayed. Meanwhile, he had stressed, he needed to raise and train the nucleus of the future army locally; he appealed for their support and asked them to contribute soldiers from among their tenants.

He felt he was fortunate to have Sir Peter Carew's help. The two men toured the district, in which of course the Carews were well known, but met with nothing like the degree of success they had hoped for. Russell wanted to raise two thousand foot-soldiers in East Devon, but the total probably never exceeded four hundred. When Russell received neither the extra troops he had been promised, nor the money to pay those he had, the men began to drift away and join the enemy in large numbers.

They did this for a number of reasons: partly because they were sympathetic to the rebels' religious principles, partly because the contest was beginning to look like a conflict between the gentry and the common people (and they themselves were sure to have scores to settle), and partly because they were not being paid and did not know when they would be. But most of all they were covering themselves. In those times it was essential to end up on the winning side, or at least not on the losing side – the punishments for that were appalling. People who were free to do so waited until they had a good idea of the way things were going before choosing sides.

For Russell, several adverse factors fed on each other: his own gloom and despondency, the non-arrival of the promised forces, the high morale of the rebels because of his inaction, the failure to recruit locally and the mounting desertions. To add to his worries, he had some pretty good evidence that his remaining men might not be entirely loyal, and an element of personal fear began to prevent him from sleeping properly. As Hoker put it:

> ... but hauing long looked for the same in vayne he was daylie more and more foresaken of suche of the common people as who at the first served and offered theire service vnto hym: and havinge but a verie small guarde aboute him he lyved in more fear than he was feared: for the Rebells dailye increased and his companye decreased and shrank awaye and he not alltogether assured of theim wch remayned.

Seventy years ago Rose-Troup had the opportunity of seeing the Petyt Manuscript, which is preserved in the library of the Inner Temple, and of comparing it with the copy Pocock had transcribed. She found that the Pocock version was full of inaccuracies and she therefore quoted the following passage from the Petyt Manuscript itself, though Pocock has been a much more common source with later historians interested in the correspondence between Russell and his masters in London:

> He complained to the Council of the problems he was having and asked them to send letters of thanks to the gentlemen for their help and asks that money be sent for distribution to their servants to improve matters. In response to this the Council sent the desired letters and authorised the payment of a hundred pounds and also sent an order to the Mint at Bristol to supply him with five hundred pounds, at the same time warning him that the rate of pay should not exceed 6 pence per day for foot-soldiers and 9 pence for light horsemen.

But he did not get the money without a good ration of further instructions and of excuses as to further delays in the reinforcements. He was given instructions about intercepting the enemy's food-supplies, on starting rumours of their devilish behaviour, of their cruelty and of the robberies they were supposed to have carried out – all to make them unpopular in the district. The Council complained that it would be hard to send in the time available the kind of force needed to defeat the rebels, but said they were preparing to send a variety of mercenaries, mostly German, Italian and Spanish. These were almost certainly intended originally for the Scottish war, and at least part of the Protector's reluctance to send such men west was because it must mean losing the impetus they had recently built up in the North. It appears that two detachments were sent on about 17 July, four-score German foot-men and four hundred 'foreign' horsemen, probably a mixture. The foot-soldiers did not get far on their journey for they were held back 'partly for the disorders of the parts hereabouts' and 'namely that they be odious to our people abroad in so much as we can hardly move them to receive them without quarrel', as the Petyt Manuscript tells us.

This unpopularity of the foreign mercenaries and the hatred with which they were regarded in the West Country turned out to be an important factor in the fighting, though it cut both ways. It stirred the rebels to fight more fiercely and resolutely, but in one or two instances their attacks were premature and unplanned because of their eagerness to get at their enemies' throats. A complicating factor was that many of the mercenaries were themselves Catholics and thus possibly suspect in this sort of rising. Hundreds of them, we are told, made it a condition of service that they should afterwards be taken to Rome for absolution for fighting on the wrong side.

But these men, whatever their drawbacks, would have been most welcome to Lord Russell had they but been there. He was still more or less alone and his morale considerably dented. He was close to being convinced by rumours that Exeter had fallen and that there was another rising of substance behind him near Salisbury which would seriously have embarrassed his lines of communication. He summoned a conference to debate the situation and allowed himself to be persuaded that the best course would be for him to retire into Dorset, advice evidently given mainly by the gentlemen from Dorset who preferred the prospect of being stationed nearer home. The decision was taken and Russell and his associates left the county and started back into Dorset.

Sir Peter Carew was always important to the king's cause in this campaign, and never more so than now. He had not been at the conference, but hearing of the outcome he was horrified. He realized at once what damage would be done to the spirits of the defenders of Exeter when they learned of a retreat when they so desperately needed an advance. He galloped after Russell, and catching up with him on Black Down, reasoned with him in the forthright manner for which he was becoming renowned. As Hoker put it: '... wheare there was a longe conference betwene theme bothe and in the ende he so perswaded the Lorde and with suche pithie reasones he carried him, that leavinge his former determinacon dothe returne againe vnto Honyton'.

But still days went past; the mercenaries – or some of them – were on the way but there were constant problems: fluctuations in their numbers, difficulties with their pay, and their unpopularity with the people through whose territory they were passing. Insurrections in Oxfordshire, Buckinghamshire and Berkshire came just at the wrong time for Russell and siphoned off men on whom he was counting.

He was more or less at his wit's end when he was called on by three men who almost certainly changed the course of local history. They were Thomas Prestwood, recently a mayor of Exeter, John Bodleigh, whose son would one day found the famous library at Oxford and whose house still stands in Exeter, close to the Guildhall, and John Perriam, who had been mayor several times. They had a number of things in common. They had all been caught outside Exeter when the gates closed, they were all supporters of the loyalist cause, and, most important of all, they were all rich merchants with good connections and good credit.

No doubt there was a patriotic element in their anxiety to help the king's cause, but it is realistic to suppose that other inducements may have occurred to them. If the rebels sacked the city they had more to lose than most in terms of property and trade. They needed a stable commercial climate to prosper and a victory for the king's men would give the best chance of that. They also no doubt had families within the walls, as well as a well-developed sense of civic loyalty and a liking for order. If the King's General was short of money, as they had heard, they could help. Hoker describes how they did so: '... and forthwth dyd procure vpon theire credytt from the merchauntes of Bristowe (Bristol), Lyme, Tawnton and ells where suche a masse of monye wch when he had received his greefe was eased'.

Now, having at last the means to do so, Russell set about raising, if not quite an army, at least a force to be reckoned with. He discovered at once how much easier it is to engage the loyalty of troops once you are in a position to pay their wages. He had just collected up his troops and embarked on drilling and training them into something like a useful fighting machine when the men and horses and guns and money so long awaited from London began to arrive.

There seems to be no way of judging exactly how many soldiers there were on either side; the available sources are suspect. Hoker speaks of 'two thousand rag and Tag rebels investing Exeter', but he was deliberately running down the enemy. Other contemporaries put the rebel numbers as high as ten thousand (the population of the city being between three and a half and four thousand). Somerset's estimate was four thousand, with less than half of them armed, but he was trying to convince Russell that he was being provided with enough men and to explain why no further expenditure was necessary. Somerset also quotes four thousand as the size of Russell's force, and this is more likely to be accurate since he would have known that Russell would be in a position to check.

In fact, the numbers of the rebels changed all the time. Before the end they were apparently able to commit between five and six thousand men to a single action after suffering heavy losses on two previous occasions, but many of these would have been country lads who had rallied to their banner only the night before. Overall it seems certain that in general the rebels had a numerical superiority and were superior in motivation. They also had the advantage of fighting in a largely sympathetic and supportive countryside, although they did not make full use of this. The king's men were much stronger in terms of training, experience, equipment, and discipline under fire; they also had cavalry. They were professionals, professionally led.

Having satisfied Russell's immediate needs regarding men, the Council felt justified in putting pressure on him to make various proclamations to the people. One interesting one concerned the property of those remaining in arms against the king. Their lands and properties would normally have been forfeit to the Crown, but the proclamation announced that such estates should become the property of the first loyal person who occupied or took them. Russell seems to have been a bit slow to appreciate the intention of this move for there is a despatch from him to Somerset complaining that he dare not make this proclamation for fear of the dissension it would cause. He did not seem to see that its intention was precisely to sow dissension and encourage rebels to rush home and check that their houses had not been taken over by their neighbours. It is an interesting comment on the solidarity of the common people that after the rising there do not seem to have been any disputes about any such annexation of property, so either Russell never got round to announcing the plan or the people scorned to take advantage of it.

There remained an element of acrimony in the correspondence between

Russell and London until he began to have real successes to report. The replies of the Council are in many cases preserved even when the letters to which they are answers have been lost. Russell was frequently taken to task for asking too much and for making difficulties considered unfitting to his long experience.

But now that he had an army Russell naturally felt he must be seen to be doing something and he decided that some reconnaissance patrolling in strength would be suitable since it would not only show the flag but would enable him to find out how things stood and whether the intelligence reports he had been receiving had been accurate. He decided to go out himself and with a moderate-sized, mobile and well-trained patrol he started out along the high road towards Exeter. But this route began to seem too risky and, fearing an ambush, he made a detour to Ottery St Mary, where he spent an uneasy night.

He had planned, in the morning, to make his way over West Hill towards the city to see at least from a distance how things stood there, but the enemy obviously enjoyed better intelligence than he had supposed, for trees had been felled to block all the roads; it would be too risky to force a way without a stronger contingent. In a fit of pique he set fire to Ottery and returned to Honiton.

He was still waiting impatiently for the arrival of Lord Grey, an experienced commander, and his troops, and for Sir William Herbert and his Welshmen. He did not want to be brought to a major battle before they joined him but he was being plagued by demands from London as to why he had done nothing. It is clear that at this time he continued to write repeatedly to Somerset asking for things, because there are replies from the Lord Protector which urge him to use his own initiative, make his own shot, and use fewer arrows (since these could be turned round and used again against his own men). The bad-tempered tone of some of these letters indicates that the Council were dissatisfied with Russell's inactivity. The rebels, on the other hand, drew comfort from it, believing it sprang from his fear of them.

About 26 or 27 July Arundell made a decision which was probably his one serious mistake: to engage the enemy in battle. Of course one can understand his reasons. His own men were feeling the effect of enforced idleness, and he knew that Russell was expecting further reinforcements shortly and had recently suffered some defections. He was right in his assessment that Russell was at the weakest point at which it would be possible to meet him. But the decision was wrong for two reasons unconnected with the actual battle that ensued. First, because the way Arundell chose forced Russell out of his inactivity, when another three or four days would surely have seen the fall of Exeter to the rebels; secondly, by bringing the enemy to battle Arundell set the pattern for the wrong kind of campaign, as we shall see.

But it is easy to be wise after the event. As it was, on 28 July a scout galloped into Russell's Honiton headquarters with the news that the rebels had advanced as far as Fenny Bridges on the River Otter and that contact had been made with them by the scouts. Fenny Bridges, then called Feniton or Veniton Bridge, is just over two miles from Honiton, but the king's army did not appear that day. Ever cautious, Russell called a council of war. The Carews urged him to try to fight the battle in the open meadow, where his cavalry could be used to full advantage, and all was set for an early start next day.

As the royal army marched through the streets of Honiton it would have been hard to deduce the feelings of the local people. For a week or two their little place had been a garrison town with the attendant advantages and disadvantages of having thousands of men imposed on a tiny population. Russell had tried hard to see that his mercenaries did not harm the king's cause by conduct which would have made them more unpopular, but it is doubtful whether these gruff, strange-sounding foreigners were ever much less than hated by any of the country people. There was no escaping the fact that the war was between good Devon and Cornish lads, fighting for the old values, and these weird, wild strangers. The people of Honiton tended to think of the inhabitants of Cullompton as pretty close to foreigners, so they are unlikely to have had much sympathy for Russell's mercenaries – quite apart from the issues at stake.

Mostly the townspeople would have kept out of the way and hidden anything of value they may have possessed. In the aftermath of a battle strange things were likely to happen, and the horsemen trotting past towards the Deer Park with their banners snapping in the breeze and the strange hairy pikemen with their loud guttural cries were certainly heading for battle.

But before they reached the crest of the rise they halted and took cover while their leaders crept forward and confirmed for themselves that down below on the water-meadows the rebels had assembled in force. Here the Otter was split into four branches with leats driving tucking-mills, to wash woollen cloth, and mills to grind corn, rather as the Exe was divided on a larger scale, outside the West Gate at Exeter.

Russell's commanders reported that the bridges were strongly held and that, while the branches of the river without bridges were not impossibly wide, the rebels had a good defensive position. Remembering Sir Peter Carew's advice, Russell instructed his captains to try to lure the rebels forward and fight the battle on ground more favourable to his own side, but the enemy did not fall for this ploy. It soon became clear that there would be no alternative to storming the bridge and forcing a way for the horsemen into the flat meadow beyond.

The Carews, eager for action and particularly suited to this kind of venture, were quick to volunteer to lead the initial assault. It had to be a headlong dash, with the horsemen prepared to go hard at the bridge and risk casualties in order to cross it at the first attempt. They went in hell for leather, sabres flashing, the drumming of hooves, the shouts, the creak and clatter of harness, the snorting of the horses all contributing to the fear that a cavalry charge arouses.

The men holding the bridge did not break, however. They stood their ground bravely, but the weight of the attack swept them aside, leaving horses, and men from both sides, struggling and broken on the trampled grass. Wan-faced, Sir Gawen Carew, who had been close behind his nephew in the van, reined his horse round after the charge using only one arm, a rebel arrow deep in the other.

The key to victory would be the quick exploitation of an early success. This Russell knew, and the moment the bridge was swept clear, even before his assault party had regrouped and begun to retire, he had the first of his foot-soldiers streaming over into the meadow. His horsemen had been invaluable for the initial assault but could not be expected to hold ground once it was taken.

Once they were in the meadow in force, the royal troops began to suffer casualties, losing men to the rebel longbows. Their commanders urged them forward for their own safety into the close-quarter fighting in which they specialized, and in which the bowmen were of little use. Their hand-guns, bills and pikes finally forced the rebels to give way and they were called off to retire towards Exeter.

Like all mercenaries, perhaps like most soldiers at that period, underpaid, brutalized, and without any higher motivation, the first thought of the victorious troops was of the spoils. They set to work stripping corpses, slitting throats here, wrenching off rings there, and generally collecting up the day's profits.

So busy were they at this absorbing task that they failed to notice Cornish reinforcements filing up and peering at them through the hedge. Suddenly a singing flight of arrows rained down on them and with fierce cries the tin miners burst through the hedge and were upon them, fighting like wild cats. The surprise was complete. Lord Russell's men fled in panic, leaving thirty or forty of their own number to add to the carnage in the field they had so recently won.

76

But of course it could not last. The trumpets of the king's army sounded again and fresh reserves, who had come from Honiton with the others but had not yet been committed to action, pressed forward. The Cornishmen were outnumbered: there were no more than 250 of them and they had cleared the field initially by a combination of utter surprise and wild determination. Hoker never liked to praise the rebels, but he was forced to admit: '... the conflict is very sharp and cruel ... the Cornishmen are very lusty and fresh, and fully bent to fight out the matter'.

Nevertheless the issue was in doubt for only a short time, and Robert Smyth, the commander of the miners, had to scramble through hedges and by sunken lanes retreat towards Exeter with a handful of limping battle-stained countrymen.

Visit it today and the water-meadow is a tranquil place, absolutely flat, heavily wooded round the edge and with a distant view of Deer Park hill over which Russell marched from Honiton. If you go to Fenny Bridges and turn into the lane that leads to Feniton, go under the railway viaduct and you are in the very lane from which the Cornishmen surprised Russell's mercenaries at their gruesome work. The hazel hedge through which they peered is as thick today as it obviously was nearly 450 years ago. The leats of the Otter ran pink that day, so legend has it. And certainly when I asked a very old lady for 'Blood Meadow' she pointed it out at once, though 'They call it Fennymead now,' she told me.

Blood Meadow, Fenny Bridges

—10—

From Carey's Windmill to the Blood-stained Heath

After making the first decisive gain of the campaign, Russell showed himself curiously indecisive again. We see this odd streak in him several times, and often enough at moments of close contact with the enemy for us to wonder whether he was physically frightened. It was never shown more clearly than in the hours after his victory at Fenny Bridges.

Having learned his lesson, he made sure that his men did not stop again to plunder the dead but pushed them on fast towards Exeter for about three miles in pursuit of the rebels. Then he called a halt and they paused, breathless perhaps after the long pull up to Streteway Head. Russell was uneasy about something. There are strange accounts of the discussions which followed. Some indicate that his jester had followed him out from Honiton and urged him to return. Others indicate that there was some panicky conversation about the bells being tolled backwards. The bells were certainly ringing, but it was in fact a saint's day and they were peacefully calling the country people to evensong. Russell did not know this, and the idea of the alarm being sounded was insidious.

The Carews and others urged him to carry on. Exeter was only about ten miles away and the rebels would still be in disarray if only he could catch up with them. But the commander was wary. He did not like the look of the country away to his left. It seemed hostile and likely to be concealing supporters of the rebels. There had again been the rumour, one that would plague him throughout the campaign, that the enemy were rising to cut off his lines of communication. Certainly the ground they were on now was perfect for ambushes, but then all Devon lanes are. Russell made up his mind. He wanted to write a number of despatches anyway, to the Mayor of Exeter and to London, in order to spread the news of his success that day. So the army turned back once more and by nightfall was again in its quarters at Honiton.

Within a few days massive reinforcements arrived: Lord Grey with a thousand experienced men from Oxfordshire and Buckinghamshire, Spinola and his 150 Italian and Spanish foot-soldiers, 200 more men released from Reading, where the disturbances were over, and a large number of German foot-soldiers. It is probable that the advance party of Sir William Herbert's Welsh troops arrived at this time also.

Now suddenly Russell felt confident; he began to believe in his capacity to defeat the rebels. He set out for Exeter in earnest and thought no more of Honiton. It had been a safe place but a place where he had waited long in frustration and indecision, so he put it behind him and headed his now impressive troops towards the besieged city.

They were nearing Ottery St Mary, probably at the tiny hamlet of Alfington, when they came under fire. Scouts came back to report that the bridge was strongly held and that the road was rampired and not easily to be passed. Spinola's Italian marksmen kept up an effective fire on any who were rash enough to show themselves over the earthworks, and a Captain Travers led a successful assault on the rampire so that the rebels had to fall back on their comrades holding the bridge. There was a brisk skirmish, but as usual the better-trained and more heavily equipped troops prevailed and the delay to the advance was short-lived.

These delaying tactics cost the insurgents little, however, and they were able to retire to a succession of ambush-points and good defensive positions. The king's men needed to engage the rebels in battle if they were to inflict any really telling losses. All this Russell knew and worried about as his men streamed through Ottery. He knew that if the rebels contented themselves with delaying tactics, with ambushes, with spirited defence and tactical withdrawal it would be hard to destroy them. There were a dozen fine defensive positions they might use before he could reach Exeter, places where they could wear down his forces, sapping their morale. And Russell's mercenaries were not best suited to that kind of warfare. They were trained chiefly for the slog of close-quarter fighting, for receiving the charge and for the counter-thrust.

Had he but known it, his opponents were to play into his hands, betrayed by the fervour of their own zeal, their natural hatred of foreigners, and blind confidence in their success. Were they not after all fighting for Christ against the Antichrist? The justness of their cause against the heretic *had* to mean something. Sadly for the rebels, what it meant was that they were to hurl themselves with insane courage into the type of conflict they could not win against battle-hardened veterans, many of whom, ironically, were of their own faith.

Because Hoker records that Russell's army passed along the byway from

Ottery St Mary and 'over the downs towards Woodbury', historians have tended to place the important battle of Carey's windmill as taking place on Woodbury Common. But at the beginning of the century Rose-Troup pointed out the unlikelihood of this. They certainly came over the down towards Woodbury, but as they had to turn right for Exeter at what is now the Half-Way Inn on the A3052 between Newton Poppleford and Clyst St Mary, they would hardly have gone on out of their way some extra miles to reach Woodbury Common. They camped, it seems certain, on what is now Aylesbeare Common and a wildlife sanctuary.

It is noticeable that Russell's force always sought a high and remote area in which to make camp overnight. A strong force in a hostile country must make this choice so that their sentries and scouts can give good warning of an enemy's approach. Smaller forces in an environment friendly to them can camp where they will. Thus the rebels tended to hold bridges and lower land, and the king's forces wilder upland sites.

On Aylesbeare Common Russell found an area of this kind and made his headquarters close to an old windmill. Nothing seems to remain of the old mill today, but one can deduce that its position was on the highest (and windiest) point of the common, close to where the Royal Society for the Protection of Birds now has a warden's caravan.

It had been a long and tiring haul up over the ridges and a lot of the more heavily armoured of Russell's men needed rest on arrival. But not all, for the Italian Spinola sought Russell out and suggested a plan to him. His men, he pointed out, were used to greater heat, were not heavily armoured and were seasoned troops. If they were to pitch their tents and order all the troops to rest for the morrow the enemy spies would soon relay the orders on. The insurgents would try to attack them in their beds, but Spinola's men would wait up for them, or rise early.

That is how it worked out. At dawn Arundell's men made what they hoped was a surprise attack. Even when it was clear to the rebels that the element of surprise had been missed, and after their initial assault had been beaten back with heavy losses, they made two or three more attacks of great determination. Arundell was at fault here, or perhaps he could not control the fury of his followers. Having failed at the first and most hopeful assault he should have held off and husbanded his resources for a better chance. Fighting round the windmill was particularly fierce and when the West Countrymen were finally and inevitably forced to withdraw they left hundreds dead and dying in the bracken.

Orders were immediately given in the king's army for a service of thanksgiving. Miles Coverdale, soon to be Bishop of Exeter but now chaplain to the forces, preached a sermon to men whose swords were still bloodstained; around them wounded soldiers and stiffening corpses lay in heaps. The mercenaries appear to have given a very mixed reception to this enforced piety, for they were of a great variety of faiths, but even before the final blessing could be pronounced it was stand to again for another assault.

This was the most extreme example of the zeal and fury of the rebels spoiling their own judgement and their own chances. It seems almost certain that their officers tried to talk them out of another suicidal attack so soon after being beaten back from the same position, but there was no holding them. Perhaps they imagined that the foreign troops would be busy despoiling the corpses as they had been at Fenny Bridges, and that they might take them by surprise again. But most of all they wanted to avenge the repulses and the casualties of earlier in the day. They were a little drunk on religious fervour and were convinced that the Lord would enable them to prevail if they threw themselves into the attack. The inevitable tragedy was repeated.

Russell doubled his guards that night, but there was no heart left in the rebels for the time being. They regrouped in Clyst St Mary and were watched from the heights by the commanders of the king's army. Russell's men could also see Exeter from their camp, so near, yet not quite within reach. They would have seen lights in the city when darkness fell and must have wondered if the people there saw them and took comfort from their closeness.

Next morning at nine Russell's army marched down towards Clyst St Mary, intent on trying the three possible entrances to the village, but the fortifications were up, and another of the spirited assaults that had been a successful feature of Russell's advance was needed.

These assaults required daring and positive leadership and Russell entrusted them to leaders, like the Carews, who had determination, dedication and a total disregard for their own safety. He was lucky to have a good supply of them. On this occasion the choice fell on Sir William Francis, the son of Nicholas Francis of Broadclyst, whose wife was one of the Courtenay daughters from Powderham. Although his own estate was at Combe Florey in Somerset, Francis was very much of the local gentry and a much admired leader of men. The attack he led at the entrance to the village, with great dash, was completely successful and the army continued, rather pleased with itself, into Clyst St Mary.

Then followed an incident which shows just how near to the surface lie hysteria and panic, even in a well-disciplined force of men. As the royal army marched on, Sir Thomas Pomeroy, one of the commanders of the rebels, found himself hiding face down in a patch of bracken while the troops swung past a few yards from him. He had with him a trumpeter and a drummer; they had become separated from the rest of their unit after the assault at the barricade. Seeing the last of the king's men go past him, Sir Thomas, on an impulse, ordered the trumpeter to sound for the advance and the drummer to beat his drum.

Convinced that they were being taken from the rear, a constant fear of an army in such terrain, Russell's men began to panic and turned and ran for the high ground they had recently left, abandoning most of their supplies and ordnance in their wild flight. By the time Russell and his officers realized it was a false alarm and had steadied and regrouped their men, Arundell's forces had picked over the abandoned guns and ammunition and carried them off to improve and rebuild the fortifications at Clyst.

None of this was lost on Russell. He knew that Clyst would be a hard nut to crack for the second time and decided that the right course would be to minimize his casualties by setting fire to the village and thus smoking out the rebels. But the approach was dangerous.

Sir William Francis again led the way along the route he had so recently stormed at such great personal risk. This time it should have been safer, but above a sunken road the attackers had to use the local men had stored great boulders and rocks, which they now hurled down on the troops below. A huge rock fell on Sir William's helmet with such force that it was driven down into his skull and he pitched forward dying. In spite of this the royal force continued to advance and set fire to the thatched roofs of Clyst St Mary. Soon all was aflame and the defenders were obliged to leave their sheltering walls. Hoker records: 'Cruel and bloody was that day for some were slain with the sword, some burned in the houses, some shifted for themselves, were taken prisoner, and many thinking to escape over the water were drowned so that there were dead that day by one and other about a thousand men.'

At the end of the village, the bridge over the Clyst was blocked. The defenders had felled two great trees across it and piled a quantity of timber against it. Worse still, they had there some of the captured ordnance, and in charge of it, if earlier accounts are true, was none other than John Hammond. He had been a thorn in the loyalist flesh at Clyst before, and in his sniping from St David's Down, and now he had newer and better guns, too. With defeat staring him in the face and with the smell of the charred timbers of Clyst in his nostrils to remind him, Hammond must have thought wryly that things could have been so different if only they had let him set Exeter on fire that short fortnight ago.

But he had little time for reflection. Perhaps word of the gunner's identity had reached the king's advance guard. Certainly Russell was having difficulty in persuading anyone to lead an assault, and Hammond's steady hand and the drift of smoke from his slow-match could clearly be seen. Russell offered a reward; no takers. Then he raised it, offering the huge sum of four hundred crowns to anyone who would attack and take the bridge. Someone stepped forward, as Hoker says: 'more respecting the gain than forecasting the peril'. He had moved only a few yards when Hammond's gun belched flame and blew him to pieces.

Then, urging the troops near the bridge to keep the defenders' attention on them, John Yard, who came from Treasbeare (near Clyst Honiton) and knew the area well, led a party secretly some distance upstream. They forded the river at a shallow point and crept silently round behind the detachment on the bridge while the advance party continued their feigned preparations for another attack. They got very close without being detected and Yard shot Hammond between the shoulder-blades as he was in the act of reloading his piece. The bridge was quickly cleared and secured.

Seeking quarters for the night, a little earlier than usual because the royal force had wounds to lick and there was no chance of reaching Exeter before dark, Lord Grey made a reconnaissance of the high land now known as Clyst Heath, above Clyst St George. There is a Heathfield Farm there now but no other visible marker to show where the final and bloodiest slaughter of the campaign happened. And slaughter, sadly, is only too apt a word.

From Clyst Heath Lord Grey is said to have looked back at Aylesbeare Common, where they had camped the night before, and to have seen the setting sun glint on armour there. Fearing an attack, and thinking that his men might be hampered by the prisoners they had with them (his detachment had charge of all those who had been taken) he ordered that all the prisoners should immediately be killed. To the disgust of the mercenaries, who disapproved of this waste of ransom money, every prisoner had his throat cut by the man guarding him, and over nine hundred were thus butchered in ten minutes.

Even the partisan historians commissioned by the winning side found it hard not to blame the king's army for this crime, but they certainly played it down and found excuses. Hayward says that the soldiers were so outraged by the unworthy actions of the rebels that they took this revenge in hot blood, but he does not go into what had provoked them. Froude tries to justify the massacre as being necessary for the safety of the army. Hoker glosses over it and, in an attempt at diversion, concentrates his venom on the poor vicar of St Thomas's, who hanged a spy but also saved Exeter from burning.

Interestingly, however, all the loyalist historians betray their own unease about the incident by their insistence that Russell knew nothing of the killings and was not even there at the time, and that Lord Grey alone was responsible for the cruel order. They were, of course, savage times, and the royal troops were obviously jittery, but, with the rebels so nearly defeated and the captives securely bound in any case, there seems to have been no real excuse for this sad blot on the reputation of the king's army.

No doubt little of this worried the soldiers as they made camp for the night, but it was an uneasy night all the same, for through the small hours rebel activity could be heard below; men and guns were being moved and digging was under way.

Arundell was planning one last attempt, and he was repeating his frequent mistake of organizing a set-piece attack when the rebels should have been defending, inflicting casualties and melting away into a friendly countryside. There is evidence that in one sense he had established firm control of his men; they would do anything for him, but only as long as they were attacking a hated enemy.

The rebels' system of intelligence was very good, and scarcely anything happened in Russell's camp that the local men did not know about within an hour or two. A report of the horrible massacre of the previous evening had reached them before dark and Arundell had difficulty in restraining his raw but furiously angry recruits from their revenge until dawn. Heart ruled head amongst the rebels, and that way might lie gallantry but certainly defeat.

At dawn a hail of shot and a shower of arrows fell on the camp from every direction, and captured guns, well sited around the camp, thundered their hideous reveille. It was a situation in which the steadiness and swiftness born of campaigning experience pays dividends which cannot be equalled by anything else. The royal troops took casualties but were soon under arms, in position and ready to ply their grisly trade.

Assault after assault was launched with reckless bravery and each was bloodily repulsed. During the action some of Russell's men cut through hedges and banks and made a way down towards Clyst St George and the Topsham road, and Russell himself led a large detachment through in a movement which cut the rebels off in the rear and made them stand at bay. Although called upon to surrender and avoid the ultimate bloodshed, they refused. We do not know who Arundell's field commanders were, but he chose well; under them the men of Devon and Cornwall, peasants, labourers, farm-workers, fought seasoned soldiers and fought them to the death.

Few things are more repugnant than the distortion or denial of the heroism of simple people. However deluded, rash or uncomprehending they may have been, the insurgents were, if nothing else, steadfastly brave.

84

It is sad therefore that so many historians hostile to the rebels' cause should have felt it necessary to demean their last efforts. The contemptuous account in Hayward's *Life of Edward VI* (written in the seventeenth century, when religious differences remained fierce) is unfortunately typical:

> Now the seditious, driven almost to dead despair and supported only by the vehemency of desire, brought forth their forces to Cliston Heath, to whom many of the most vile resorted hourly, which much enlarged their numbers, but nothing their strength. The Lord Grey encouraged his men to set sharply upon the vulgar villains, good neither to live peaceably, nor to fight, and to win at once both quiet to the Realm, and to themselves glory. So he brought the King's forces upon them rather as to a carnage, than to a fight, insomuch as without any great either loss or danger to themselves, the greatest part of the seditious were slain.

Hoker, however, could not bring himself to distort the truth that far, and was reluctantly forced to admit that: 'Valiantly and stoutly they stood to their tackle, and would not give over as long as life or limb lasted, yet in the end they were all overthrown and few or none left alive.' He then quotes the views of the callous and hardened old soldier Lord Grey, who had seen years of active service in many theatres of war and was not at all easily impressed: 'Great was the slaughter and cruel was the fight and such was the valour and stoutness of these men that the Lord Grey reported himself that he never in all the wars he had been in did know the like.' This seems a fair tribute from an enemy.

−11−

The End of the Siege

Strangely, in these last desperate days, when the relieving forces were getting closer and closer to Exeter, those in the city seemed to be worse informed than they were before Russell reached the area. Perhaps he was too heavily involved in the fighting or the planning to keep up his normal steady flow of reports and letters; perhaps the intensified pressure made it harder for his messengers to smuggle information in.

Within the walls they knew the fighting was going well for their side and they had heard about the very heavy losses of the rebels, but from their own standpoint nothing seemed to have changed, except that the starvation was even more acute. There were still large numbers of rebels camped round the city, and the noise, activity and harassment continued unabated. It was encouraging to have news of victories and promises of relief within days, but there was no other indication that salvation was really at hand, and no certainty that they themselves would survive even a few days longer. Indeed, each day it seemed that they might not last until tomorrow.

Until the last twenty-four hours of the siege the determination and unity of the citizens was surprisingly sound. The majority of those who might from choice have thrown in their lot with the rebels on religious grounds either supported the mayor out of civic loyalty, or decided to keep quiet and see how things would go. But there had been one ugly incident. Looking back on it, Mayor Blackaller realized it had been a mistake, one he would not repeat, but it had seemed a good idea at the time. He had summoned all the commoners to a rally outside the Guildhall, because he had thought that getting everyone together would emphasize their unity, and hoped to build up their morale with a fine speech. But as the crowds gathered it occurred to many of those who remained openly or secretly loyal to the old religion that they were in a considerable majority.

Woodcut of the siege of Exeter from an account 'by an unknown chronicler'

Some of them saw it as an opportunity to get the Catholic supporters to commit themselves to the rebel cause. Thinking to start a riot for this purpose, and to pay off an old score, a clothier called Dick Taylor put an arrow to his bowstring and let fly at his particular enemy. But somehow he tangled his hand in the string, and the arrow flew wide of its intended mark. To Dick's horror it hit his best friend, the Controller of Customs, John Peter. By a lucky chance it struck one of his ribs; otherwise it would certainly have killed him. (Hoker gives the additional information that Taylor eventually died in a debtors' prison, making this sound like divine intervention, although his fate might of course have been the natural financial consequence of poor judgement, in view of how he behaved on this occasion.) History does not record what the mayor said or did to him, nor whether John Peter remained his best friend after he had recovered from his injury.

In the last days of the siege, when it looked as if either sedition or starvation would prevail, a hundred of the staunchest hearts and chief men of the city banded together in a strange brotherhood. This measure was partly self-denying, in that they agreed not to take part in sallies, which were then thought damagingly excessive; partly investigative, in that they vowed to seek out signs of treachery and keep watch on enemy tricks and espionage, and partly supportive, in that they assigned themselves to extra patrols and rampart duties, helping and checking on the guards. They also made a solemn pact that, if the city should be forced to yield, the brotherhood of one hundred would meet at the postern gate by Bedford House to escape together or to die together, fighting in the Crolditch.

As in all tense situations in war, a lot depends on the example shown by prominent people, and here it is hard to over-emphasize the splendid contribution of John Blackaller, the chief citizen. He seems to have been everywhere and coped with everything. He settled disputes, organized rescues, looked after the poor, maintained morale, calmed down the over-excited and generally kept the peace in a most difficult and explosive situation.

Not everyone else's example was as good. Hard times can mean increased profits, and all wars produce their profiteers. Such a one was Nicholas Reve. A rich man who wanted to be richer, and a member of the honoured 'Chamber' or council of twenty-four who ran Exeter, Reve was a brewer. He thought it likely that the stresses of the siege might actually stimulate the demand for ale, but there were other brewers, and in order for his plan to succeed he needed their co-operation. He persuaded most of them to join him in putting up the prices when no cheaper brew could be brought in from outside. One of the brewers, however, either an enemy or a patriot, informed the mayor, and there was an inquiry. Reve was not only fined heavily but expelled from his influential place on the council.

Quite the opposite was the behaviour of an elderly character whose name has not come down to us. He was something of an eccentric by all accounts but endeared himself to the poorer people by throwing open his storehouse and sharing its contents with them. Naturally this move was a popular one, and it also seems to have made a difference to the food situation, perhaps because the old man had stored up a lot of food. He was prone to making somewhat flowery loyal speeches which might have been less convincing if he had not backed them up with his selfless sharing. In one such peroration he announced that, if necessary, he would eat one of his arms while fighting with the other before he would allow the city to yield to the rebels.

The mayor's excellent care of the poorer people was another important factor. The poor were obviously very vulnerable to all emergencies, having no reserves of food or money, but they were also a potential source of unrest, being those most likely to agitate for surrender. With all this in mind, no doubt, Blackaller ordained that cattle seized on raids outside the city would not belong entirely to those who took them, but were to be divided up on a municipal basis, and he ensured that the greater part of the meat went to the less affluent. He also arranged assistance for them in another way, as Hoker records: '... there was a general collection set and rated throughout the whole city for their relief: and thereby they were liberally every week considered: which thing being some increase to their stock and store was the better to their content: all such victuals as were to be had within the city they either had it freely or for a very small price'.

The mayor seems to have had a reputation for fairness to the poor as well as for his care of them during the siege. Much of the church silver was sold at this time, partly to improve the lot of the poorest citizens and partly to pay the wages of the soldiers who were in the city. Blackaller even insisted that, when there was a windfall, such as captured cattle, some of the food went to the prisoners in the gaol under the Southgate tower, though when the situation became desperate they had to be content with horseflesh, which Hoker tells us they eventually grew to like.

Although there had been no time to provision the city against a siege, records show that there were some supplies in the warehouses. Hoker again: 'Albeit theare were good store of drye fishe, rice, prunes, raisons and wine at very reasonable prices', which indicates that a ship or two from Spain or Portugal had probably berthed a few days before hostilities commenced.

The most serious shortage was of bread, which was consumed in large quantities in the sixteenth century, especiaily by the poorer folk. When the wheat flour finally ran out the bakers had to turn to the really hard famine measure of baking 'horse bread'. This was the poorest kind of dough, made from whatever could be procured: corn, beans, peas, bran, anything. In some places such loaves were regularly made by bakers, famine or no, but only for animal feed. The problem was that by the nature of the ingredients the dough would not set or stick together during the baking. As a contemporary account tells us: '... in this extremity the bakers and householders were driven to seek up their old store of puffyns and bran wherewith they in times past were wont to make horse bread and to feed their swine and poultry and this they moulded up in cloths for otherwise it would not hold together and so did bake it up and the people well contented therewith'.

Well contented or not, even the horse bread was exhausted near the end and the city was within a hair's breadth of being surrendered through hunger. All the mayor's good leadership and busy organization could hardly have postponed that event much longer.

When news of Russell's successes and the heavy rebel losses at Aylesbeare Common reached the city, and it was reported that the king's men were near Clyst, within walking distance of the gates, the spirits of the townspeople rose and their minds were taken off their hunger for a while. But the news also stirred those who really hoped for a rebel victory. There seems to have been communication between the besiegers and their supporters in the city, for on the final Sunday of the siege, which was raised on the morning of Tuesday, 6 August, a last desperate assault was made upon the gates, timed to coincide with troubles within.

The attackers concentrated their efforts on the South Gate, even though it was massively fortified, because the greatest number of their sympathizers lived in the South Gate area and there was more chance of this gate being opened to them, they considered, than any of the others.

The trouble started at eight in the morning on that last Sunday, when Catholic supporters, according to Hoker, 'gadded up and down the streets'. They were under the leadership of John Vincent and John Sharke, and were 'walking with their weapons and armour as to fight with their enemies'. They began chanting inflammatory slogans, hoping to start a riot. Hoker quotes them as shouting: 'Come out you heretics. Ye two-penny book men [a reference to the new prayer-book]! Where be ye? By God's wounds, by God's blood! We will not be penned in to serve your turn. We will go out and have in our neighbours. They be honest and Godly men.'

The rebel sympathizers knew that they needed a major diversion to give them a chance to get the great gates open – hence the taunting. But it was to no avail, for the majority of the loyalists were either at church or at breakfast, or had been well warned by the mayor not to fall for such a ploy. He himself was quickly on the scene, and with the magistrates managed to get most of the people to their homes quietly.

But not quite all. Some of them tried to pick a fight with the guards at the South Gate in the hope of getting it opened. Our resident chronicler describes the fracas in Southgate Street: '... there was a little stir which being soon stopped, there ensued no hurt thereof other than a broken pate or two'.

So the last rising in the city came to nothing, either because it came too late or was not fully supported. The Catholic faction was far from resolute. No doubt the widespread horror of the crime of high treason – and the punishment attaching to it – had something to do with it. Hoker, as usual, knew exactly why things turned out as they did, and which side had the support of the Almighty. In the end the troubles came to nothing because, he believed, 'The Lord kept the city'.

The terrible losses at Clyst Heath sealed the fate of the insurgents. Arundell had found that his brave peasants, even when they gave their all, could not be a match for seasoned soldiers. They had tried again and again and each time they had been bloodily repulsed. Now they barely had the strength to keep up the siege and the victorious Russell would be down the

Topsham road and at the gates within twenty-four hours. It might still be possible to fight one, or possibly two delaying actions, extending the siege by a day, even a day and a half. But to what purpose? They would not be able to hold Exeter if it fell to them. It would be empty of food and its munitions would be nearly exhausted. Besides, his men were on their last legs.

But there was something else; something Arundell and his officers had not spoken of in the last few days for fear of lowering morale. Huge numbers of wild Welshmen under Sir William Herbert were pouring down the Bristol road and might be there as soon as Russell was. From the London road too there came reports of reinforcements for the loyalists. A council of war was called. Overwhelmingly, excepting a few gentlemen who knew they had more to lose than the peasants when the reckoning came, the council clamoured for dispersal, for retreat to the West, whence they had come; to the West, where the roads still lay open.

In the bitter silence of defeat, of high hopes muddied underfoot, they packed camp and stole away, leaving the walls unguarded and the citizens unaware that they were free to come out. It was, in fact, the gentlemen confined in the tower of St Sidwell's who first discovered that the rebels had gone. With no warders to stop them they broke out before dawn and pounded on the East Gate. Nobody took any notice of them at first – there

The tower of St Sidwell's Church, where Walter Raleigh senior and others were imprisoned. The church was destroyed by German bombs in 1942.

had been too many false alarms – but eventually they were able to convince the guards of their identity and were taken to see the mayor.

As often happens, the delirium of sudden freedom led to wild excess, or, as Hoker described it:

> The sound and comfort whereof was so great and the desire of fresh victuals so pierced that many not abiding till the daylight gat and shifted themselves out of the gates but more for victual than for spoil ... and yet they were glad of both: howbeit, some did not long enjoy the same, for many being more greedy for meat than measureable in feeding did so overcharge themselves in surfeiting that they died thereof.

The paintings of Hieronymous Bosch come to mind, and no doubt it was a scene of grotesque excitement and activity, quite apart from the horror of those who ate themselves to death. In any case, such was the confusion that no one seems to have thought of telling Lord Russell. He marched out early on 6 August. To his surprise he met no resistance on the roads and was nearly at Exeter before he found out what had happened.

Russell's army approached the city along the Topsham road, past what is now County Hall, dipping temporarily out of sight at the bottom of the Hollow-way (now Holloway Street), swinging right at what is now the Artillery Inn and across to Southernhay. The parade was dazzling to the townspeople and the army appeared very splendid. The mayor, however, sent word begging Russell not to bring his men in as there was no food at all. For this reason they camped in the open ground outside, where the rebels themselves had been ensconced for the past weeks. Russell established his headquarters in St John's Fields. He would no doubt have liked to repair to the superior comfort of his own house, Bedford House, inside the city, but deferred to the mayor's wishes in the matter.

There seems to have been a great reception for the civic authorities and a banquet set out in tents in Southernhay, but the army was kept outside the walls for three days until the city felt ready to entertain them. Then Russell was formally and lavishly welcomed. Unfortunately Hoker is silent on this interesting time. Possibly he was too busy with official duties to keep up his diary.

Then a thousand of the Welsh troops arrived. They were evidently seen as a mixed blessing. There are numerous reports of the good work they did helping to revictual the city, though on a very commercial basis; but there are also many references to their rapacity. Hoker, restored to activity, sarcastically wrote:

Sir William Herbert, the Master of the horses and after the Earl of

Pembroke, came with a thousand Welshmen: who, though they came too late to the fray, yet soon enough to the play, and too soon, as some thought, for in spoiling they wereso cruel as most insaciable: howbeit in this they were very courteous, for what they could not carry with them they were content to leave behind.

There were a number of colourful accounts of the Welsh helping themselves but one should remember that they were probably fuelled by resentment that the newcomers had not suffered the dangers and deprivations they had. Spoils in return for the rigours of battle was fair, but these Welshmen, who were almost as much foreigners as the mercenaries to the Devon men, had turned up fresh, cheerful and unmarked but still expecting their share.

A document in the Exeter municipal archives relates an incident in St Stephen's Church: '... a chalice weighing by estimation xv oz or thereabout was taken from the said church in the commotion time after my Lord of Bedford came to the city by a Welshman who went into the church and locked the clerk in the church ... and went away with the chalice'.

What seems certain is that the Welsh soldiers came to the starving city at the right time, with the resources to obtain and sell food at a good price, and profited from the situation. The account we find in the *Holinshead Chronicle*, as revised and extended by Hoker in 1587 – the same year as his production of the earliest known printed map of Exeter – is quite specific: 'But the city being as yet altogether destitute of victuals, and the Welshmen at their first coming seeing the same, they did by their special industry and travails fraught and furnish the same within two days with corn, cattle and victuals, very plentifully, to the great relief and comfort of the people therein, and to the benefit of themselves'. Hoker's tone here can be seen to have moderated amazingly since his first bitter outburst against the Welshmen, which was probably a reflection of popular indignation.

These days were widely known as the 'commotion times' and certainly a lot of people other than the incoming soldiery were intent on feathering their nests. A lot of church silver disappeared in most suspicious circumstances and the excuses offered were not always convincing. One man who was alleged to have been given a chalice belonging to St Edmund's Church to look after denied it. When it was discovered that he did have the chalice he claimed that he had found it under his bed during the 'commotion times'.

St Sidwell's probably suffered the most. The rebels seem to have respected this church, even though it was in their power during the seige, but, afterwards, we are told: 'In the commotion time the church was spoiled of all things moveable in a manner save only a pix, a paten, two cruets, and four bells whereof one Bernard Duffield took away three which he hath not restored neither can we tell where he hath them'. This is the same Bernard Duffield who was cast into gaol for his intransigence during the siege, the father of the fiery Frances who slapped the mayor's face. He was certainly one to take advantage, as did many others, of the opportunities offered by the troubles.

Even the gentry seem to have been less than totally scrupulous about the ownership of property at this time of free for all, and one sympathizes with the patient administrators trying to unravel the rights and wrongs of all the conflicting evidence. A group of those gentlemen who were imprisoned in St Sidwell's Church took it upon themselves to ensure the safety of the church's silver, although in the event it was not always quite as safe as it should have been. Raleigh's father and a few others placed a quantity of silver in William Slocum's house 'for safe keeping'. But Slocum said he gave it to Thomas Chapel and it was taken by John Bicker and Richard Wallys, from whom, it was claimed, it went to Sir Roger Bluett. This gentleman may have been aptly named for the parishioners had difficulty in regaining the silver, we are told, 'because they could not come by Sir Roger'!

They also asked Walter Raleigh to return a bolt of cloth of rather special quality. One might have expected that gentleman to be embarrassed at being unable to comply, but not a bit of it. He answered them coolly: 'That they should have it back if it were not cut already for the sparver [curtains] of a bed'.

Meanwhile the victorious Russell was fully occupied at his favourite task, writing interminable reports on the success of his campaign and on the need for more money and more troops. He apparently kept aloof from the turmoil in the city, content that the spoiling of the churches and any other depredations could conveniently be blamed on the rebels, and otherwise on the Welsh – a point of view swiftly accepted and widely promoted by the Privy Council in London.

—12—
Rewards and Revenge

Amongst his other duties, Lord Russell had been charged with rewarding the good and punishing the bad as he saw fit, except that certain key figures were to be brought to show trials in large towns, or in the capital itself. There were also cases in which he needed the Privy Council's sanction, or at least the king's confirmation afterwards by letters patent. In general he had been advised to punish leaders, especially the gentry, with great severity and to let the common people go home if they showed contrition and a resolve to loyalty in the future.

Russell seems to have imagined that the rebellion was entirely over and that all he now needed to do was settle the accounts. At any rate, between 6 and 16 August he gave no thought to the possibility of further fighting and set to work to balance the books in Exeter. As a result, the leaders of Russell's army did well for themselves. Sir Peter Carew gained a large part of the Wynslade estates in Buckland Brewer and other places; Sir Gawen was given most of Humphrey Arundell's lands. William Gibbs was presented with the estates of John Bury at Tavistock and Plympton. Richard Reynell of East Ogwell was rewarded with the demesne of Weston Peverell and a house called Pennicross near Plymouth. The mayor and corporation of the city of Exeter received the manor of Exe Island as a memorial of their staunchness and fidelity. Russell himself, Herbert and Grey, the chief leaders, received large grants, mainly of land, all over the county.

Russell divided his energies between reward and revenge and Hoker tells us that he had 'forches and gallows' set up in various places and caused many to be put to death 'especially such as were noted to be chief doers and busy ringleaders in this rebellion'.

Revenge was also taken against the popular and tough little vicar of St Thomas's, who a few weeks before had stopped Hammond from using red-hot shot to burn down the city during the siege. It is strange that Robert Welsh should have been singled out quite so soon for revenge. Perhaps his very popularity made it necessary to make an example of him as a matter of urgency. He had certainly been a chief supporter of the rebel cause, but always openly and honestly, and his saving of the city might have been expected to win him a measure of mitigation. But he probably had enemies with old scores to settle. His execution was entrusted to the ruffian Bernard Duffield, who had seen the inside of several prisons and would later make acquaintance with more. He seems to have accepted the task with revolting enthusiasm.

The vicar was to be hanged from the tower of his own church, St Thomas Becket, which stands across the river from the West Gate and was then outside the walls. Hoker seems to have been present at the occasion and has left us his account of it. Duffield, he tells us:

> ... caused a pair of gallows to be made and set up on the top of the tower of the said vicar's parish church of St Thomas and all things being ready and the stage perfected for the tragedy the vicar was brought to the place and by a rope about his middle drawn up to the top of the tower and there in chains hanged in his popish apparel and having a holy water bucket, a sprinkle, a sacring bell, a pair of beads and such other popish trash hanged about him and there he with the same about him remained a long time. He made a very small or no confession but very patiently took his death.

The corpse swung on the gibbet at the top of the tower (as a grisly reminder to the people) for several years; in fact, according to Jenkins' *History of Exeter*, it remained there until the accession of Mary Tudor.

Meanwhile Russell kept his pen busy and the messengers to London and elsewhere fully employed. He wrote suggesting rewards and knighthoods, expressing his thanks, forwarding petitions and generally helping to set things in order. He asked the Privy Council for more men and money. The money he got, but he was told to release men, especially horsemen, who were needed elsewhere as there were now real threats of a French invasion. He was also told to get on with the campaign and finish it.

This infuriated him. He thought it was ungrateful and unreasonable, for he had assumed the campaign was over. It was therefore even more of a shock when, a day or two later, he heard that a thousand or so rebels under Arundell had formed up again at Sampford Courtenay and were apparently looking for trouble. This news reached him on 16 August.

Quite why the rebels, repeatedly defeated already, should want another

The execution of Father Welsh

show-down with Russell's army, now reinforced and far larger than their own, is hard to work out. Possibly it was genuine religious zeal. They would certainly have been better advised to disappear, the leaders abroad and the others into anonymity, but this they were not prepared to do. They felt that they were committed to a holy war.

Russell set off for Sampford Courtenay on 16 August, and found the rebels strongly entrenched outside the village. With Sir William Herbert in command of Russell's advance guard, the first fortified barrier was attacked and overwhelmed, but the defenders were able to fall back on their supporting groups. Sir William pressed on, perhaps a little hastily, for he seems to have left Lord Grey and the second echelon some distance behind. At that point a large contingent under Humphrey Arundell himself launched a flanking attack at the rear of the attacking soldiers. The unexpectedness of this bold move threw the royal troops into confusion for a while, but Grey, coming on the scene just in time, rallied the rearguard and gradually the superior numbers and skill of the professionals began to tell. Arundell's men were forced to withdraw, still in fairly good order but with quite heavy casualties.

There was another desperate fight at the end of the village, where the rebels had stretched a great chain across the road – a favourite device of those with most to fear from cavalry – but the final outcome was beyond real doubt. Hoker's words again underline the gallantry and determination of the local men, especially when we remember that he normally lost no opportunity to play down their exploits: '... they would not yield to no persuasions nor did, but most manfully did abide the fight and never gave over until that both in the town and in the field they were all for the most part taken or slain'.

One of the Welsh captains, Ap Owen, fell here, as did Underhill, one of the original Sampford Courtenay leaders. He had proved himself a good soldier, for a village tailor, having commanded the Sampford contingent from the very beginning. A few escaped to Okehampton, Arundell and the younger Wynslade amongst them.

This time Russell changed his established pattern of caution after a victory and pressed on in hot pursuit. He may have been nettled by the implication in Somerset's letter that he tended to hang back when he should have hastened on – always an insulting insinuation to a soldier – or more likely he felt for the first time absolutely secure in giving chase. The rebels were now badly mauled, and he had a stronger force than ever before.

The retreat turned into a rout. From Okehampton up on to the moor Russell's horsemen hunted and killed. Contemporary accounts suggest 700 rebels killed and as many more taken prisoner. And more killing there would have been if night had not overtaken them, bringing Russell's party at least a very uncomfortable night.

He himself records that he spent a miserable night in the saddle because they found themselves in strange and unfriendly country and expected a rebel counter-attack at any moment. It is hard to believe that there was any realistic chance of such an attack, in view of the crushing defeat inflicted only hours before, and it seems strange that not even the general himself was able to dismount. Either Russell found himself cut off from the main party of his troops with just a handful of horsemen, or he was exhibiting a personal nervousness which would in turn explain certain other of his apparent excesses of caution.

The shattered remnants of Arundell's force needed that dark night to fall back on Launceston for their last stand, but this never really took place. There was some sort of disturbance in the town and Arundell, with William and John Wynslade, Maunder, and Bowyer, Mayor of Bodmin, was overpowered. Here he learned the heart-breaking news that Kestell, his trusted secretary throughout the struggle, had been in the pay of Russell all along, and had been keeping the Lord Privy Seal posted of all Arundell's movements and plans. He and the other leaders were secure in the castle dungeons before Russell's men even arrived.

Within a few days they were transferred to Exeter, on horseback, hands bound behind them and feet lashed beneath their horses' bellies. Across the wilds of Dartmoor the melancholy party trekked, then down through villages, in most of which a grim reminder of the folly of their treason hung from a gibbet. And then across towards Exeter, past the church of St Thomas, where the rebels' once brave and cheerful companion and supporter swung in his creaking chains overhead. How bitter to Arundell was the jeering of the people by the roadside, who until a few days before would surely have cheered him. As always he was haunted by the spectre of the revolting death that awaited him. When they arrived in the city, the prisoners were lodged in Rougemont Castle. The dungeon doors slammed and they heard the rattle and stamp and chatter that meant doubled guards and no chance of escape.

In a surviving memo to the Lord Privy Seal written around this time, the Lord Protector is most congratulatory about Russell's successes and instructs him to bring Arundell, Maunder, the mayor of Bodmin and two or three 'of the most rankest leaders of them here to be examined and after to be determined of as shall appertain'.

But there was still some clearing up to be done. A thousand rebels were said to be in Somerset, possibly heading for Minehead. Sir William Herbert and his Welshmen were sent up the Exe valley, through the sleepy hamlet of Bickleigh (home of another member of the Carew family) and then, Rose-Troup tells us, by the old road along the top of the ridge towards Bampton.

Near Tiverton, at Cranmore Castle, Herbert caught up with some rebels who were prepared to fight. He captured several and summarily hanged and quartered them. A larger group were overtaken at King's Weston in Somerset; exhausted, dispirited and heavily outnumbered, they were badly mauled and more than a hundred were taken, including two of the leaders: a gentleman called Coffin, and John Bury, both of whom were brought to Exeter.

By the end of August it seems likely that Russell had left the far West for Exeter. Gaps in the correspondence make it impossible to prove this, but the fact that he had by then appointed a Provost Marshal in the Field (to execute the Cornish rebels with sufficient severity to inspire terror in people's hearts) supports the supposition, since this appointment was clearly a substitute for his own presence. In choosing Sir Anthony Kingston as Provost he made sure of the severity, but also of the lasting hatred of every Cornishman, for this detestable man made a sport out of a grim task and exercised his twisted sense of humour in a sickening way.

In his *Chronicles*, Grafton, a contemporary writer, tells how Kingston, having decided that the mayor of Bodmin was guilty, wrote to the mayor to say that he and some important guests were coming to Bodmin and would appreciate lunch. The mayor arranged a lavish meal. Just before they ate, Kingston took the mayor aside and told him that there had to be an execution and would he please arrange for the construction of a gallows, to be ready at the end of the feast. The mayor gave the necessary orders and all sat down to the food and wine. At the end of the meal Kingston asked to be shown the gallows. 'Are they strong enough, do you think?' he enquired. When the mayor assured him that they were, he was told: 'Then climb up to them, for they are for hanging you'.

Another example of Kingston's gallows humour was shown when he had hanged the wrong man, the miller's servant instead of the miller himself. A passer-by protested to Sir Anthony that he had hanged the servant, to which he replied: 'And so? Could he ever have done his master a better service than to hang for him?'.

Kingston repeated his 'coming to lunch' joke on the Portreeve of St Ives at the George and Dragon Inn there, and throughout Cornwall built up a reputation for tasteless inhumanity. Even Hayward, no friend to the rebel cause (and indeed a frequent distorter of the truth in the loyalists' favour), asserts in his *Life of Edward VI*: '. . . Kingston was deemed by many not only

100

cruel, uncivil and inhumane in his executions ... nor did they trouble themselves to discern between the loyal subject and the rebel, making profit of both indifferently'.

He was certainly one of the most gratuitously cruel men of a cruel age. On one occasion, coming upon a crowd at a cemetery, Kingston found that there was a grave and a corpse but that the parson would not conduct the service until some disputed dues were paid. He therefore had the priest thrown into the grave and buried alive. Such was the universal detestation of this despised but feared man, we are told, that in some parts of the county the common people would spit on the ground at the mention of his name a century after his death.

Kingston remained violent and untrustworthy to the end of his life. In 1555 Mary Tudor consigned him to the Tower on suspicion of treason, but soft-heartedly listened to his lies and became convinced she had misjudged him. He was therefore released but within a year was deeply implicated in the Dudley plot to depose Mary; he was given the task of raising the people of the West Country against her and persuading them to march on London – a curiously inept choice!

At different times, in a career longer than he deserved, Kingston was arraigned on charges of adultery, consorting with coiners, and trying to rob the Tower of London. Having finally been arrested, he was being brought to London under escort when, on Henley bridge, he suddenly and brutally spurred his horse over the parapet in an attempt at either escape or suicide. As his name appears on a register of prisoners drawn up at the Fleet a few days later he must have been rescued from the Thames, though he died before he could be brought to trial, thus robbing the hangman of a truly poetic piece of justice.

One wonders at the scorn with which those who controlled events must have regarded the Cornish. William Body, the Commissioner charged with the implementation of the new religious regulations before the Western rising, made himself so offensive that the Cornish could scarcely imagine anyone worse. But they found one in Kingston, a man who certainly plumbed the depths of viciousness and cruelty.

At about this time the Duke of Somerset's power began to run out. The faction in the Privy Council led by the Earl of Warwick, sensing that their time was coming, took advantage of all of Somerset's errors and misfortunes. Although the reasons for Somerset's fall are also tied up with the state of the country as a whole, it was his handling of the Western Rebellion that finished him. He was accused of being too lenient, even of sympathizing with the rebels. He was certainly indecisive and fussy, and ironically it was these qualities that alienated Lord Russell, who could be accused of precisely the same failings himself. When Russell withdrew his support, the Lord Protector surrendered, and was imprisoned. He was eventually executed in 1552.

Russell seems to have left Exeter for London on about 26 or 27 September. Before he left he appointed a Commission of Five to maintain order in the West and to attend to anything further needed in the way of rewards and punishments. The first problem he left them with was one he himself had realized was too hot to handle.

On 12 September the Privy Council had written ordering him to arrange the removal of all the bells, except the smallest of the peal, from every church in the two counties. Only the churches in the city of Exeter were exempted. This was intended as a ritual punishment or mark of disgrace, and had been done elsewhere in England and in other countries. The idea behind it was that the bells had often been rung, sometimes backwards, as a warning of approaching troops or as a means of calling the people together. Bells were very expensive and would not easily be replaced even when allowed to be, and in those very religious days the loss of the church bells affected all the people.

Anticipating trouble from these instructions, Russell had immediately modified the plan so that the bells would be taken down but left in the safe keeping of some local worthy. Even this provoked such antipathy that the Commission of Five watered down the plan even further and in general took away only the clappers, ensuring that the bells could not be rung. As a result the Church Goods Inventory of 1551 shows that almost all Devon churches at least had their full quota of bells. At St Sidwell's, however, outside the walls of Exeter, the dreadful Bernard Duffield personally took away three bells, and no doubt made a profit from them. The bells of the West Country remained silent until Mary came to the throne, then they rang in jubilation, reflecting her popularity – though it was to prove short-lived.

Most of the contemporary sources play down the gravity of the rebellion, diminish its importance and minimize its effect. Reading them one would not imagine that anyone in London had felt threatened. But from some of the records not intended for posterity one learns otherwise. Towards the end of July, when the outcome of the troubles in the West balanced on a knife-edge and rumours of the fall of Exeter were heard daily, the Council was in a state of dread. When the reports of the rising in Norfolk were added that dread became little short of panic.

Scores of cannon of all sorts were brought from the Tower armoury to add defensive strength to the gates of the city. Proclamations warned all Londoners to make ready their weapons and their armour. The bridge at

Staines which carried the main road from the West was actually demolished, and the Lord Mayor started to prepare the city for war: he himself helped to check up on the alertness of watchmen, and the readiness of guards and alarm signals, at night.

On 8 September Arundell and his companions wound in despairing procession through the gates of the city; eleven men, heavily outnumbered by their guards, ten of them with heads bowed from the fatigue of riding with hands and legs tied. Close by each prisoner rode a horseman with cavalry sabre at the ready. Instructions from London on the transmission of the prisoners made it clear that if any rescue attempt was made during the journey the prisoners were to be killed:

> ... when you send up the prisoners we do not doubt but you will send them up strong enough and if any attempt should be to deliver them out of your hands, you will give them that bring the prisoners such charge that rather than they should be enforced to lose them than make them first sure of escaping that they may give account of them to us quick or dead.... .

Three days earlier they had ridden down the road that skirts Fenny Bridges and could have seen traces of the battle if they had had the stomach to look. Every crossroads in the West would have had its gibbet with the foul remains of some fellow rebel revolving slowly to a change in the wind. And now, riding over London's cobbles, the prisoners were taunted by the jeers and obscenities of the crowd.

Arundell, Pomeroy, the two Wynslades, Wise, Harris, Coffin, Bury, Holmes and ffortescue: they were a sad party. The eleventh man rode apart from the others and his hands were free although his face was troubled. He was Kestell, the false secretary to Humprey Arundell and Russell's valued spy. He had come to give evidence and did not much relish the prospect.

Arundell, Bury, John Wynslade and Holmes were taken to the Tower, Pomeroy, William Wynslade, ffortescue, Wise and Harris to the Fleet prison. Of Coffin there is no further documentary trace. He may have died of wounds, or been released. The other five were released from the Fleet on 1 November by order of the Privy Council. On the face of it this seems curiously clement by the standards of the time, but they may have surrendered voluntarily and were probably heavily fined in any case.

By the time the remaining four came to trial, Somerset himself was in custody and this may account for the delay that occurred before they faced their accusers in Westminster Hall. As was the custom in those days at treason trials, none of the evidence was committed to paper, but Arundell,

John Wynslade, Bury and Holmes were duly found guilty of high treason and condemned to be taken back to the Tower and later: '. . . to be drawn on hurdles through the city of London to the gallows at Tyburn and on that gallows suspended and while yet alive to be cast down upon the ground and the entrails of each to be taken out and burnt before their eyes while yet living and their heads cut off and their bodies to be divided into four parts to be distributed at the King's pleasure'.

Having heard those dread words they went down again to the waiting barge, their escort commanded by the Constable of the Tower, and drifted downstream to their prison again, entering by the Traitor's Gate this time. They must surely have known then, for news travels fast in such places, that Somerset was also lodged somewhere inside the grim establishment that kept them.

On 27 January 1550, after a two-month wait, all four started on the terrible journey by hurdle to Tyburn tree. Nothing could really mitigate the horrors of the traitor's death they suffered, though their pride in undergoing what they regarded virtually as religious martyrdom may have helped them a little. Within an hour the brutish crowds had departed and the four heads and the bloodied limbs had been impaled on the rusty spikes that decorated the gates of the city.

The Western Rebellion of 1549 was over, and paid for.

Bibliography

The main source must be the contemporary account of the rebellion as presented by John Vowell (John Hooker, *The Description of the City of Exeter*, ed. W. J. Harte and others, Devon and Cornwall Record Society, 1919–47). Vowell, alias Hoker or Hooker, was chamberlain to the mayor of Exeter and present in the city throughout the siege. Most of the local detail in this book is owed to him, and a good deal of the immediacy of the story, but he wrote for the side he was on and is often not objective.

The secondary contemporary source is the letters and despatches of the Privy Council and Russell, though not many of Russell's letters have survived (*Troubles Connected with the Prayer Book of 1549*, ed. N. Pocock, Camden Society, 1884).

The principal secondary source is Frances Rose-Troup's major work *The Western Rebellion of 1549* (Smith, Elder & Co., 1913). This very thorough book is marred by diffuseness and sentimentality but still deserves the attention of any serious student of the uprising.

Other works that I have found valuable or interesting include:

S. Baring-Gould, *Book of the West* (Methuen, 1899)
Blake's *Rebellion of Cornwall* (reprinted Royal Institute of Cornwall, No. 56)
Carew's *Survey of Cornwall* (ed. Halliday, Andrew Melrose, 1953)
Sir J. Cheke, *Heart of Sedition* (London, 1549; reprinted Oxford, 1641)
J. Collier, *Ecclesiastical History* (1708)
Cotton and Wollacombe's *Gleanings from Exeter Records* (Exeter, 1877)
Fisher's *Political History of England*
Foxe's *Acts and Monuments* (1563)
Froude's *History of England*
Gairdner's *English Church in the Sixteenth Century*
Grafton's *Chronicles* (1568)
Grafton's *Proclamations*
Hayward's *Edward VI* (1630; Camden Society, 1840)
Hibbert's *Dissolution of the Monasteries*
Holinshead Chronicle (1578, reprinted London 1807–8)
Hook's *Lives of the Archbishops of Canterbury* (1875)
Hughes, P. L. and J. F. Larkin (eds), *Tudor Royal Proclamations* (New Haven, 1964)
Izacke's *Antiquities of the City of Exeter* (London, 1736)
Alexander Jenkins, *History of Exeter* (Hedgeland, Exeter, 1806)
Latimer's *Sermons*

Sir John Maclean, *Sir Peter Carew* (Bell & Daldy, London, 1857)
George Oliver, *Bishops of Exeter* (William Roberts, Exeter, 1861)
——. *Ecclesiastical Antiquities* (W. C. Featherstone, Exeter, 1846)
——. *History of the City of Exeter* (1861)
Pollard's *Protector Somerset*
Richard Polwhele, *The History of Cornwall* (Facsimile, Cockell & Davies, London, 1803)
J. Prince, *Worthies of Devon* (Exeter, 1781; reprinted London, 1810)
A. L. Rowse, *Tudor Cornwall* (Macmillan)
Smith's *English Guilds*
Speed's *Chronical*
T. Westcote, *A View of Devonshire*, G. Oliver and Pitman Jones (eds) (Exeter, 1845)
R. N. Worth, *A History of Plymouth* (Plymouth, 1872)

Index